Clear

Understandings

Clear
Understandings
A Guide to
Legal Writing

Ronald L. Goldfarb
and
James C. Raymond

RANDOM HOUSE · NEW YORK

Grateful acknowledgment is made to the following for permission to reprint previously published material:

West Publishing Company: Reprinted with permission from 19 Federal Rules Decisions, page 235. Copyright © 1957, West Publishing Company.

Library of Congress Cataloging in Publication Data
Goldfarb, Ronald L.
Clear understandings.
Includes index.
1. Legal composition.   2. Law—United States—
Language.   I. Raymond, James C., 1940–
II. Title.
KF250.G64   1983   808'.06634   82–40147
ISBN 0-394-70634-X

Manufactured in the United States of America
98765432
First Edition

Acknowledgments

We wish to thank all of the lawyers and judges who were our students in the writing courses we taught during the last ten years; many of them really were our teachers at the same time. We also thank our colleagues on the faculty who taught this legal writing course, particularly Dwight Stevenson and Gypsy De Silva, for sharing their ideas and their experiences with us.

We are indebted to our friend and colleague Frances Michael for the sane and competent and friendly fashion with which she handled all of the administrative and clerical work regarding this manuscript, and to Gail Ross for her assistance.

We are grateful to Henry Carlyle for suggesting the title of this book.

Ronald L. Goldfarb
Washington, D.C.

James C. Raymond
University, Alabama

Contents

Introduction:
Let's Kill
All the Lawyers

According to Fred Rodell, the brilliant, cantankerous, iconoclastic late professor of law at Yale, "There are two things wrong with almost all legal writing. One is its style. The other is its content."[1] Rodell's point was that the language of the law often creates a smoke screen in which logic is lost and meaning mangled. As a result, legal language may cause disputes and provoke lawsuits, instead of preventing them.

Rodell's attack on the language of the law, especially his book *Woe Unto You, Lawyers,*[2] was considered blasphemous by his colleagues in legal and academic circles when it was made decades ago. He was dismissed as a rogue, a hyperbolic rebel. But in his career of lecturing and writing about law, especially about the U.S. Supreme Court, Rodell proved his point better by example than by polemic. In popular magazines and newspapers—*Fortune* and the *New York Times*, for example—he wrote about what previously had been viewed as strictly legal subjects, fit only for scholarly journals, in a way that was clear and engaging to the general reading public. In so doing, Rodell demonstrated a fact of literary life that novelists have known and have profited from—that the law provides a rich lode of subjects for the good writer and the intelligent reader.

Rodell had his admirers, of course, more than a handful, many of whom took his course on legal writing, a once-a-week afternoon seminar conducted in a public room Rodell reserved at Mory's Tavern around the corner from the law school. For one who took this offbeat elective course, it had no equal for intellectual stimulation and sheer fun. But it was hard work, too. It demonstrated the rigor and the rewards of painstaking writing. And it also established a truth that we wish to demonstrate in this book: that good writing is more than an aesthetic exercise, though surely it is this, too; good writing aids the thinking process, and therefore affects the substance of what is written. Careful, clear writing prevents confusion; clumsy, slipshod writing causes conflicts. For lawyers, and for their clients, nothing could be more critical.

The modern American journalist whose work best exemplifies Rodell's lessons is Anthony Lewis, whose writing about the law in the *New York Times* is widely praised. His book *Gideon's Trumpet*[3] about a criminal case from its inception to its resolution in the U.S. Supreme Court is a classic example of legal writing that is technically accurate enough to satisfy knowledgeable lawyers and at the same time engaging enough to satisfy lay readers.

There are other well-written books on the law published for the benefit of lawyers and general readers. An example is Charles Rembar's *The Law of the Land*,[4] whose introduction is so polished that we read it aloud for the delight and edification of students in our seminars. Mr. Rembar is a practicing attorney. Edmond Cahn, the late New York City law professor, wrote probing analytical books about legal philosophy—such as *The Moral Decision*[5]—but did so in an engaging and readable fashion. Sybille Bedford's *The Faces of Justice*[6] is an insightful and perceptive view of four countries' legal systems. Neither an attorney nor a legal scholar, Bedford has written books about law that are wonderfully revealing even as they are eminently readable. Several specialized newspapers for lawyers have emerged in recent years—the *National Law Journal*, the *Legal Times* of Washington, and the *American Lawyer*; these are serious publications with a critical viewpoint, but are all written with the stylistic grace that made Rodell so accessible and influential.

Still, the general press provides too little good coverage and analysis of the law. And the hundreds of law journals and the thousands of judicial opinions published each year continue to purvey turgid legalese, while practicing attorneys crank out reams of badly written documents full of legal lingo that no educated writer should respect, no decent editor print, and no client tolerate.

The best cure for legalese is a healthy dose of Holmes, Cardozo, and other eminent stylists who have written about the law in literature or have written law so brilliantly that it qualifies as literature. In 1960, Ephraim London published a two-volume anthology, *The World of Law,*[7] illustrating a tradition of excellence in legal writing "from Biblical times to the present." Volume I, *The Law in Literature,* includes examples from Dickens, Balzac, Lewis Carroll, Chekhov, Twain, Sholom Aleichem, Maugham, Auchincloss, and O. Henry—to name just a few. Volume II, *The Law As Literature,* includes accounts of notorious cases, famous testimony, judgments, and reflections on the law by such writers as Shaw, Camus, Wilde, and Mencken, and by lawyers and judges such as Holmes, Jackson, Hand, and Frank. London's collection demonstrates what Rodell preached: it is not necessary—in fact it is diversionary—to invent a legal argot in order to tell a legal story in truth or fiction.

More recently, in England, a similar pair of books was published by Louis Blom-Cooper, with literary examples ranging from Plato to Camus, along with selections from famous lawyers and judges throughout the English-speaking world, from Francis Bacon to Felix Frankfurter.[8] These books and others like them are persuasive exhibits in support of our thesis: that legal style can be technically precise without the shackles of needless jargon and pompous diction.

Why are lawyers, who like to think of themselves as hard-fact people, so often attracted to literary language, sometimes to defend themselves for not producing it, sometimes to argue that they have in fact written literature? The reason, we think, is that *language is, if not the substance, at least the vehicle of both trades,* and that lawyers and literati are bound to regard each other with the admiration and alienation of any natural siblings. The best attorneys, like the best literary writers, are people who are both possessed by language and in complete control of it; they won't rest until they have served it and it has served them. There are drudges in both trades; but there has never been a great attorney or a great literary writer whose work did not give as much pleasure as understanding.

In the chapters that follow, we will attempt to show attorneys and future attorneys what the problems of legal writing are and how they may be solved. Our observations are based not only on our individual experiences as a practicing attorney and a professor of English but also on a decade of teaching writing to state trial and appellate judges, federal administrative law judges, government attorneys, and others in the legal professions. We do not pretend that every lawyer who reads this book will emerge as a skilled writer; that would be as foolish as promising to make a pianist of everyone who reads a book on piano playing. Unlike other consultants in the field, we are wary of formulas for testing and improving style. We have tested the formulas themselves, and, as we will show, found them wanting. For us, writing is a fine art, and though instruction helps, it is no substitute for practice, for trial and error with the assistance of teachers; for a certain amount of talent, and for ambition and self-discipline. Still, we think that what we offer here will be useful to all attorneys or law students who want not merely to survive but to excel.

thus The point of the book (if anyone has failed by now to notice) is that lawyers do not need a separate language; indeed, it is wrong and troublesome not only for them but for their clients when lawyers imitate the style that they must have, in their innocence, at one time detested. Books and articles about the law and the legal process, by lawyers or by anyone else, do not need legalese. More important, in their everyday work—writing letters, memoranda, briefs, laws, opinions, and other documents—lawyers should learn to think like professional writers, since that is precisely what they are.

Although attorneys and future attorneys are our primary audience, nonlawyers—clients and the general public—have a stake in our thesis too. Rodell explained why:

> Certainly a man who enters a business deal of any kind, whether he is buying a radio on the installment plan or setting up a trust fund to take care of his family, would seem entitled to know, to his own complete intellectual satisfaction, just what he is getting out of it and just what he may be getting in for. The legal document he signs won't tell him. Certainly a man whose democratically elected government enacts a law which will regulate him or tax him or do him a favor would seem entitled to know, if he wants to know, exactly how the new statute is going to affect him. His lawyer may "advise" him—and may be right or wrong—but reading the statute won't tell him. Certainly a man who loses a lawsuit would seem

entitled to know why he lost it. The court's opinion won't tell him. Why? Why doesn't and why shouldn't legal language carry its message of meaning as clearly and fully as does a cookbook or an almanac or a column of classified advertisements to anyone who wants to know what ideas the words are intended to convey?[9]

Why indeed. The answer is as various as lawyers are various. In some cases the motive is insecurity, in some cases incompetence, in some greed. In most cases, we hope, it is because lawyers have just never considered the other possibilities. If they continue in their druidic isolation, the only course lay people might have is what Dick the butcher, in *Henry VI, Part Two,* suggested: "The first thing we do, let's kill all the lawyers." To which Jack Cade, the visionary rebel, added, as if anticipating our theme, it is "a lamentable thing . . . that parchment, being so scribbled o'er, should so undo a man."

From Shakespeare's time to recent national surveys measuring the popularity of various professions, lawyers generally have had a bad reputation. Today the American public holds a grudge against the half-million counselors who handle its legal affairs. There are many reasons for this: lawyers often bear bad tidings and fight other people's bitter battles; they are often needed at times of stress and become associated with the problems and the clients they are attending; too often they are mischievous, incompetent, and exploitative. But one reason lawyers suffer a bad public image—the reason we are interested in discussing and one that easily could be avoided, to everyone's benefit—is their atrocious and pretentious prose.

All professions—doctors, architects, sociologists, athletes—have their own gibberish and jargon, which they understand perfectly when they speak among themselves. Lawyers too have their jargon, but the public has an interest, often an obligation, to understand what lawyers write.

Therefore, lawyers have special obligations to communicate beyond their own group. They charge generously for their writing, so it should be clear and correct. They deal with highly personal, important, and vital social problems. The stakes are high. Matters of real substance—life and death and commerce and human relations—depend on the correctness and accuracy of legal writing.

There is a related problem, one of image, which relates legal language to lawyer unpopularity. When a paying customer with a lot at stake does not understand the gibberish he is agreeing to, he resents the counselor who drafted the language and urged its adoption. Pompous, ponderous, arcane language does not impress most clients; it annoys and affronts them, as a rule. It leads people to conclude that lawyers like to use mumbo jumbo to create a phony mystique, to dominate situations, and to enable them to charge fees which are as outrageous as their language.

It need not be this way. The atmosphere is right for reform. In the late 1970s and early 1980s, increased attention has been paid in state and federal governments to what has been dubbed the "plain-English movement." Former President Jimmy Carter issued an executive proclamation requiring all federal regulations to be written so that common folks could comprehend them. State officials have taken similar steps, and six state legislatures (New York, Maine, Connecticut, Hawaii, Minnesota, New Jersey) have passed laws requiring major institutions that deal extensively with the general public—banks and insurance companies, for example—to write their forms and agreements in simple, straightforward language.[10] Several other states are considering adopting similar laws. This movement should have a salutary effect on what might be called action documents, contracts and wills and other everyday legal prose that are constrained by their subject matter from reaching the heights that lawyers might aspire to in the articles, reviews, editorials, and books they write about the law.

The law is lively, interesting, and important; the language of the law should reflect this reality, engaging and serving consumers and participants in the legal system. A law professor made this point recently in a review:

> Lawyers work with words and ideas and seek to arrive at decisions and characterizations by argument and persuasion. The best legal education is one that cultivates this art at the highest intellectual and moral level and in that way encourages the best advice and the best decisions.[11]

This is what our book is about. Our philosophy is based upon our perception of how the law functions in society: it attempts to bring stability, order, and justice to social behavior in large part by putting understandings into words on paper. What makes this enterprise difficult is that language and the conventions that govern its representation on paper are at bottom arbitrary, often illogical, inherently ambiguous, and constantly changing. We are not so naive as to believe that the "rules" editors and schoolteachers talk about are absolute and immutable laws, like those that govern the motions of physical bodies. On the other hand, we acknowledge a phenomenology of language that lawyers cannot afford to ignore, a body of conventions, however subjective, that educated readers customarily rely upon, not just in judging whether a piece of writing is "correct," but in inferring what the writer was trying to say. We are not so naive as to suppose that lawyers should write like journalists or novelists, or that their prose should always be entertaining as well as instructive. On the other hand, we are persuaded that lawyers who have distinguished themselves as great writers have in common with other good writers certain techniques, certain resources, certain sensibilities to the nuances of language that enrich the law, not encumber it, making its expression both pleasurable and precise.

Our philosophy, in a nutshell, was best expressed by Sydney Greenstreet, playing a wily underworld character in *The Maltese Falcon*. Striking a deal with Sam Spade, the crafty detective (Bogart, of course), Greenstreet lifts his glass in a toast: "Here's to plain speaking and clear understanding."

We offer his sentiment as a toast to the legal profession.

Clear
Understandings

1

Legalisms, Latinisms, and Macaronics

Something strange happens when human beings enter law school. Perfectly normal, usually intelligent, and relatively sophisticated people begin what can only be called a process of intellectual brainwashing. Few who are exposed recover. John and Joan Jones become L. Jonathan or J. J. Jones. They exchange their jeans and jogging jackets for pin-striped suits. They learn a foreign language called legalese.

Soon after entering law school the Joneses get the notion that to be lawyers, they must learn to speak and write like lawyers. The straightforward language that has gotten them through life up to then no longer issues from their lips. No one actually tells law students that learning legalese is required to pass the bar, but they inevitably get the message by some perverse osmosis.

By the end of three years of law school, John and Joan can barely get through a letter or a conversation without dropping a few "notwithstandings," "heretofores," and "arguendos." Everything they have read and heard for three years—the hornbooks, casebooks, reported cases—is loaded with legalese. Law journals, the staple diet of law students, are full of articles bearing bombastic titles and subtitles; are weighed down by footnotes galore; and are characterized by writing in which, Rodell has said, "a pennyworth of content is most frequently concealed beneath a pound of so-called style." By graduation, Mom and Dad don't recognize their son or daughter. Like Lamont Cranston, the fictional hero of radio's *The Shadow*, J.J. has learned "a strange and mysterious way to cloud men's minds."

As neophytes who want to be accepted in the legal establishment and are afraid to be different, most young lawyers sink deeper into the bad writing habits they have learned. Whether it is because they are unsure of themselves intellectually or because they are enjoying their sudden status, they have bought the bilingual brief. If they join a prestigious law firm they are unlikely to begin writing memoranda or briefs different in style from what they see around them. They coin long words and pepper their writings with foreign cant and stuffy phrases, and the vicious cycle continues.

If the Joneses have learned their lessons well, after graduation they may be hired by large corporations to write agreements like this one, which was once used by the Ford Motor Credit Company in the state of Washington as part of its standard contract with customers:

> In the event Buyer defaults in any payment, or fails to obtain or maintain the insurance required hereunder, or fails to comply with any other provision hereof, or a proceeding in bankruptcy, receivership or insolvency shall be instituted by or against Buyer or his property, or Seller deems the Property in danger of misuse or confiscations, or Seller otherwise reasonably deems the indebtedness of the Property insecure, Seller shall have the right to declare all amounts due or to become due hereunder to be immediately due and payable and Seller shall have all the rights and remedies of a Secured Party under the Uniform Commercial Code, including the right to repossess the Property wherever the same may be found with free right of entry, and to recondition and sell the same at public or private sale.

Or they may be hired by an insurance giant to create policies that read like this:

> If total disability occurs during the grace period for payment of a premium, such premium shall not be waived, nor refunded if paid, provided that failure to pay such premium within the grace period therefor shall not of itself invalidate a claim hereunder for total disability commencing during such grace period if such premium with

compound interest at the rate of 5 percent per annum is paid at the time due proof of the claim is furnished by the Company.

If they are scholars and not of a practical bent, J.J. and Jonathan may choose to remain in the womb of their alma mater, becoming professors themselves and earning their stripes by publishing books that read:

> It may be possible to delineate the limits on magnitude better than we have done, but the foregoing should suffice to illustrate the basic idea: in deciding the magnitude of the scale, deterrence may be considered within whatever leeway remains after the outer bounds set by a scale of a certain magnitude has been chosen; however, the internal composition of the scale should be determined by the principle of commensurate deserts.

They may eventually become judges, and be spared the obligation of writing *anything* original, conspiring instead with attorneys, abetted by form books, to dispense justice in prepackaged language:

> This cause coming on to be heard was submitted upon Bill of Complaint, Answer of Defendant, and testimony taken in Open Court with both parties represented by Counsel; and upon consideration thereof, the Court is of the opinion that the Plaintiff is entitled to the relief prayed for in part in her complaint.
>
> It is therefore ORDERED, ADJUDGED and DECREED by the Court, that the bonds of matrimony heretofore existing between the Plaintiff and Defendant be, and the same are hereby dissolved and the said is forever divorced from the said for and on account of INCOMPATIBILITY OF TEMPERAMENT.

Occasionally lawyers have confessed to confusing their clients with malice aforethought. "Clients won't pay fees for legal papers they can understand," a candid practitioner once reported. "But if I fill them up with Latin phrases, wherefores, and hereinafters, they feel they're getting their money's worth and they pay. . . . I recently filed a request for a rule nisi. Now how could I ask my client for a $5,000 fee if the Latin word *nisi* were changed to the English unless? The whole proceeding seemed far more impressive to him with a Latin title."[1]

And a Florida legislator was overheard opposing a bill that would have required plain English and simplified forms in realty contracts. If this law passed, he would have to reduce his legal fees for real estate closings back home, he feared. The bill was not reported out of committee.

Whatever the causes, whatever the motives, the writing style of lawyers has several idiosyncrasies, the most obvious of which are legalisms, Latinisms, and a peculiar word game akin to macaronics —the medieval verse form in which poets switched playfully back and forth between Latin and the vernacular. Less obvious, though no less perverse, are solipsisms (prose that only the writer can understand), solecisms (sentences that not even the most ingenious grammarian can disentangle), and technical jargon borrowed from scientists and engineers.

A legalism, according to Arkansas Supreme Court Justice George Rose Smith, is "a word or phrase that a lawyer might use in drafting a contract or a pleading but would not use in conversation with his wife."[2] Had he written his definition today, Judge Smith might have used "his spouse or hers" instead of "wife," but the definition is as sound now as it was in 1967. To Smith, legalisms are as absurd and unnecessary in the law as they are in ordinary conversation. To illustrate his point, he has us imagine a lawyer at the dinner table saying, "I can do with another piece of that pie, dear. Said pie is the best you've ever made." And another lawyer who says, "Sharon Kay stubbed her toe this afternoon, but such toe is all right now."

One subset of legalisms consists of Latin phrases used where ordinary English would serve as well. We are not talking about ordinary phrases like *bona fide,* or those for which there are no obvious phrases in English, like *habeas corpus.* We are talking about *res ipsa, capias, arguendo, vel non, ore tenus, ex contractu, ratio decidendi,* and similar phrases used to give legal writing a learned air even by attorneys who could not distinguish a *scintilla* from a *seriatim.* Our favorite example is by a Canadian judge who was genuinely learned, and who liked to pretend that his readers were too. As a legal principle, he cites this maxim, which he calls a well-known presumption:

> Benignae faciendae sunt interpretationes, propter simplicitatem laicorum, ut res magis valeat quam pereat; et verba intentioni, non e contra, debent inservire.

The meaning of this maxim is that judges should be generous in interpreting legal documents written by nonlawyers, since the laity does not know much about the law—a condition not likely to improve if judges keep their secrets in a foreign language. We find it difficult to imagine the audience for whom this passage was intended, since it appeared in a published opinion without translation. We never suspected the existence of a colony of Romans north of the St. Lawrence.

Lawyers generally defend legalisms by calling them terms of art. Every profession, they argue, has them. "Carburetor" may be jargon to nonmechanics, but we cannot for that reason expect mechanics to say "the gadget that mixes air and gasoline" whenever they want to refer to a device that has a useful name of its own.

We agree. But we distinguish between terms of art that are legitimate because they have no equivalents in ordinary English and terms of art that are vestigial and should be stated plainly. Phrases such as "equity jurisdiction" or "tenant at sufferance" are to the lawyer what "carburetor" is to the mechanic. Even Latin is acceptable in legal style in such phrases as "prima facie" or "stare decisis," but only because there are no economical English equivalents. But there is no excuse for "inter alia" when "among other things" would serve as well, or for "same" in place of an ordinary pronoun.

Because contemporary law has vestiges of Latin, French, Anglo-Saxon, and even Celtic, lawyers are given to a peculiar kind of prolixity called iteration, the habit of saying the same thing two or three times in different words, often in different languages. Lawyers feel obliged to write both "will" (Anglo-Saxon) and "testament" (Latin)—not that one attorney in a hundred could tell you if the two terms are legally distinct. Lawyers who are not sure whether one "grants" real property and "bequeaths" personal property are likely to write that their clients give, grant, bequeath, and devise the property, throwing in all the words they can think of, hoping that one will hit the mark.

Lawyers alone find the need to cease as well as desist, to transfer not just a right, but a title and interest as well, instead of choosing one word to describe what they mean. An appellate judge who disagreed with the trial court in a contempt case declared the conviction "reversed, vacated, and held null and void." A colleague on the bench suggested that he add "and stomped on."

James B. Minor, an attorney turned writing teacher, took the lawyer's love of iteration to its logical and absurd conclusion in this sentence, which we do not find particularly farfetched:

> We respectfully petition, request and entreat that due and adequate provision be made, this day and the date hereinafter subscribed, for the satisfying of this petitioner's nutritional requirements and for the organizing of such methods as may be deemed necessary and proper to assure the reception by and for said petitioner of such quantities of baked cereal products as shall, in the judgment of the aforesaid petitioner, constitute a sufficient supply thereof.

That, Minor says, is how a lawyer might say "Give us this day our daily bread."

A simple test for distinguishing necessary from unnecessary jargon is to try to express the concept economically in the sort of language you might use with an intelligent listener in polite company at dinner. If you can say it in plain English, do not make yourself more boorish on paper than you would at the dinner table by showing off your command of language unfamiliar to your audience.

As the law becomes increasingly specialized, new possibilities for legalese develop, so that lawyers can make themselves incomprehensible to one another as well as to the public at large. When lawyers have mastered narrow specialties, they often distill them into a shorthand that makes no sense to nonspecialists who are obliged to read it. Thus a lawyer who has divined the government's policy toward taxing capital gains can let the rest of the world in on the secret in a passage like the following, which we chose at random from the *IRS Federal Tax Regulations* at §1.211–1(b) (3)(ii)(1975):

> In determining the transitional additional allowance deductible as provided by this subparagraph, there shall be applied thereto in full on a dollar-for-dollar basis the excess of net long-term capital loss over net short-term capital gain (computed with regard to capital losses carried to the taxable year) to the extent that the long-term capital losses carried to the taxable year from taxable years beginning before January 1, 1970, as provided by 1.12121–1(b) and subdivision (iii) of this subparagraph, exceed the sum of (a) the portion of the net capital gain actually realized in the taxable year (i.e., computed

without regard to capital losses carried to the taxable year) which consists of net short-term capital gain actually realized in the taxable year exceeds the total of short-term capital losses carried to the taxable year from taxable years beginning before January 1, 1970, as provided by 1.1212–1(b) and subdivision (iv) of this paragraph.

The problem is not limited to tax laws. This is how the regulations of one Western state explained a parole-board rule enacted for the benefit of inmates seeking release from prison:

Parole Release Date

254–30–032 (1) The Board shall set a parole release date within the parameters of the matrix in Exhibit C unless it finds aggravation or mitigation under rule 254–30–033, or the statutory good time date on the sentence imposed is shorter than the matrix range. In the latter case, the parole release date set shall be set at six (6) months *less than* the statutory good time date on a sentence of up to three (3) years; *at* nine (9) months *less than* the statutory good time date on a sentence between three (3) and six (6) years; and at twelve (12) months *less than* any sentence exceeding six (6) years, unless the Board makes a finding pursuant to (2) of this section.

Variations from the Ranges

254–30–033 (1) The Board may depart from the parameters of the matrix only upon making a specific finding that there is, by a preponderance of the evidence, aggravation or mitigation which justifies departure from the ranges. The Board shall clearly state on the record the *facts and* specific reasons *for* variation from the range.

We call this solipsistic writing—writing that would be appropriate if the writer were the only person expected to understand it. Its cause is the writer's overfamiliarity with the subject matter. Having mastered the intricacies of a finite field, the writer either forgets the viewpoint of the person who has not mastered the area, or refuses to make the necessary concessions to that viewpoint.

Attorneys writing for the Occupational Safety and Health Review Commission (OSAHRC) have a particularly specialized practice; almost every case they handle is governed by a single act of Congress. They have become so familiar with this act that they have converted it to a new language, which we call OSAHRCian. Instead of communicating in words, OSAHRCians communicate in numbers and letters that presumably are clear to other OSAHRCians. A memo from one OSAHRCian to another is likely to read:

> Pursuant to 29 U.S.C. §661(i), respondent asks the Commission to vacate a citation for violation of 29 C.F.R. §1926.105(a); because of the present composition of the Commission, 29 U.S.C. §661(e) bars the appeal.

To OSAHRCians the memo is perfectly clear: an employer has been issued a citation for not providing a safety net, and the Review Commission, with one seat vacant, cannot muster enough votes for acquittal. To the rest of the world, however, including the general-practice lawyer who might defend against citations like this only once or twice in a career, the memo is gibberish.

Every attorney who has researched a case thoroughly has trouble resisting the impulse to write as if the reader ought to know the material as well as the writer does. Consider this opening statement:

> This is an application by way of originating notice brought pursuant to S. 4 ss 1 of the Municipal Conflict of Interest Act, 1972, for a determination of the question of whether or not C. and H., both trustees of the O. Board of Education, have contravened the provisions of Subsection 1 of Section 2 of the said Act.

This of course makes sense to anyone who has memorized the local Municipal Conflict of Interest Act of 1972. The OSAHRCian equivalent of this opening is found in a memorandum in which the duty of the commission was set forth in these unequivocal terms:

> The following issue is presented to the Commission for determination:
> Did respondent violate section 5(a)(2) of the Act by failing to comply with 29 C.F.R. §1926.750(b)(ii) or 29 C.F.R. §1926.105 in the alternative, and 29 C.F.R. §1926.750(b)(ii)?

We can imagine the response of a weary commissioner who is greeted by such a salvo on a sleepy Friday afternoon. The Honorable Wilbur F. Pell, Jr., of the U.S. Court of Appeals for the Seventh Circuit cites an equally soporific beginning from what would seem to be a typical brief:

Is Rule 121.538(a) of the Code of Federal Regulations an Order within the ambit of 49 U.S.C. 1486 solely to grant exclusion jurisdiction in the court of appeals?

The writer no doubt meant "exclusive" rather than "exclusion." But even so, Judge Pell says, such beginnings remind him "of the *New Yorker* squibs, captioned 'Letters We Never Finished Reading.' "[3]

The New Yorker, by the way, has published an all too credible passage on "language" from a form used by the Maryland Transportation Authority, which, the magazine tells us, is an example of "The Bureaucratic Mind at Work." It is a compendium of everything lawyers ought to avoid:

GP 1–1.07 LANGUAGE

In order to avoid cumbersome and confusing repetition of expressions in these Specifications, it is provided that whenever anything is, or is to be done, if, as, or, when, or where "contemplated, required, determined, directed, specified, authorized, ordered, given, designated, indicated, considered necessary, deemed necessary, permitted, reserved, suspended, established, approved, disapproved, acceptable, unacceptable, suitable, accepted, satisfactory, unsatisfactory, sufficient, insufficient, rejected, or condemned," it shall be understood as if the expression were followed by the words "by the Engineer" or "to the Engineer."[4]

Another nasty habit lawyers have is using a negative phrase to make a longer-winded positive statement (or assertion, as it might be called). Something justified is "not without good cause," and knowing something is to be "not unmindful" of it. This foible becomes more problematic when one or more negative statements are strung together with one or more positive statements to create verbal algebra, requiring the reader to keep a careful tally of pluses and minuses to determine what the message might be. A classic example is this constitutional amendment that voters in one Southern state encountered in very small print next to a lever on their voting machines:

No moneys derived from any fees, excises, or license taxes, levied by the state, relating to registration, operation, or use of vehicles upon the public highways except a vehicle-use tax imposed in lieu of a sales tax, and no moneys derived from any fee, excises, or license taxes, levied by the state, relating to fuels used for propelling such vehicles except pump taxes, shall be used for other than cost of administering such laws, statutory refunds and adjustments allowed therein, cost of construction, reconstruction, maintenance and rights-of-way, payment of highway obligations, the cost of traffic regulation, and the expense of enforcing state traffic and motor vehicle laws.

Notice the complex string of negatives ("No moneys . . . except . . . and no moneys . . . except . . . shall be used for other than"). This structure would be tough to follow in a short sentence; in a sentence 107 words long, it is an insult to the electorate, a mockery of the notion that voters deserve to have a voice in deciding how their taxes are spent.

Here is the same problem in briefer span, a sentence written by an attorney whose job it is to keep university administrators abreast of the law:

Dismissal of a claim by faculty members that a university had violated their constitutional right to free speech after they protested the university's adoption of an increased student-faculty ratio was improper, the federal court of appeals in Philadelphia has ruled.

There's nothing wrong with this sentence if you have the time to read it two or three times. Once you get to "improper"—a negative statement—it becomes obvious that what was improper was a "dismissal"—a negative action—and then you can figure out that it was a "claim" that was dismissed, not a faculty member, and that the dismissed claim was that a university had violated the faculty's constitutional right to free speech *after* they protested something about an increased student-faculty ratio. This information should be very useful to college presidents who need to make quick judgments in similar circumstances.

Here is another example of confusing negatives in which an Idaho judge gives a continental twist to an otherwise perfectly opaque observation:

The propriety of considering the counsel's submittal dehors the record is obviated by the Court's determination that it is unnecessary to show that the demand by the plaintiff must be equal to or less than the award of the jury.

Sentences like this one are common in legal writing. We are still not sure what to make of the following, written by a judge in one of our seminars:

> Counsel inform me that the defendants plead that the signature on the deed being a forgery was not defective by reason of the signature having been obtained through trick, artifice, fraud or false pretenses.

What, we wonder, was not defective? The forgery, the signature, or the deed? This is a solecism—a puzzling grammatical construction that yields no logical meaning, or any number of meanings. Another example is this sentence, in which an insurance company seems to defend itself by refusing to provide a defense:

> The complaint is forwarded to the defendant insurance company who does not provide a defense claiming the allegation of battery does not fall within the terms of their coverage and they, therefore, have no obligation to defend.

Another common fault of legal writing has to do with the fact that lawyers, like professionals in almost every field, are often lured by the jargon of scientists and engineers, as if briefs and opinions could be made more authoritative by the hard, objective, impersonal style of technical English. The first requirement of this style is that human beings may not be used as grammatical subjects. The effect, presumably, is to suggest that what is being reported is not what someone has observed or opined, but what actually *is*. By using the structure Rodell called the "backhanded passive" (as in "it would appear" and "it is suggested that"), lawyers imagine themselves to be avoiding the appearance of subjectivity as well as avoiding personal responsibility for judgments that are ineluctably subjective. Of course their names usually appear elsewhere on the page.

Here are a few examples we have discovered in our work with various state and federal agencies.

> It is requested that the Commission authorize the use of compulsory process.

> Thus, it was held by the bankruptcy judge that the Commission did not have a claim which was provable under the Bankruptcy Act.

It is our belief that they have been run locally within the past three months.

There was an inability to complete the construction on schedule.

"It" and "there" used in constructions like these are dummy subjects—artificial stand-ins for the persons or things that are responsible for the action in the sentence. With only a little coaching, lawyers can be emboldened to say who did it right up front: "I request," "the bankruptcy judge held," "we believe," and "the builders could not."

A closely related problem is the unnecessary use of the passive voice. The passive voice has legitimate uses and good writers use it with some frequency, but bad writers use it without control. In fact, most of the attorneys we have instructed do not even know how to distinguish the active voice from the passive.

So we remind them. In the active voice, the grammatical subject performs the action named by the verb (for example, "John sued Mary"). In the passive voice, the grammatical subject receives the action named by the verb (for example, "Mary was sued by John"). Notice that the passive voice is two words longer than the active voice, and that it shifts the reader's attention from the doer to the recipient.

The passive voice is appropriate when a writer has reason to focus attention on the receiver of action. Otherwise, good writers avoid the passive voice when they can, partly because it is uneconomical and therefore less direct (the passive *always* requires two more words than the corresponding active construction), and partly because it tempts the writer to achieve a false economy by suppressing information that the reader might want to know (e.g., "Mary was sued"—but we won't say who did it). In support of a budget request, one attorney wrote that "staff development and training is repeatedly identified as one of the foremost concerns of correctional practitioners." Converting this sentence to active voice not only would improve the style but would also require the writer to say who identified this concern, which ought to have been important information for the reader who had to make budgetary decisions.

We do not go so far as to say that the passive voice is always wrong or inappropriate; we say only that writers ought to consider the effect of an active-voice construction before settling for the passive. To illustrate the damage the passive voice can do, we cite a narration of facts from an opinion, first as it was actually written by one of our former students, Justice Robert H. Miller of the Kansas Supreme Court, and then as we rewrote it, changing each of Judge Miller's active constructions to passive. Anyone who reads the two passages aloud will concede that Miller's version, the one on the left, is far superior.

The record discloses a run-of-the-mill tavern brawl. Werkowski and a friend, David Bolduc, were patrons of the King's Knight Tavern in Derby, Kansas, on May 4, 1974. They were playing pool. . . .

The state presented evidence that Bolduc spilled beer on the pool table; he gave unsolicited advice to others who were playing pool; and he repeatedly and unnecessarily asked Kendall Wooten, another patron, to move out of the way. Wooten finally refused. Werkowski then waved his pool cue at Wooten and said, "This will make you move." Wooten took the cue from Werkowski, laid it down, and then proceeded to shove Bolduc out the door.

A run-of-the-mill tavern brawl is disclosed by the record. The King's Knight's Tavern in Derby, Kansas, was being patronized by Werkowski and a friend, David Bolduc. Pool was being played by them.

Evidence was presented by the state that Bolduc was "obnoxious": beer was spilled on the pool table; unsolicited advice was given by him to others by whom pool was being played; and Kendall Wooten, another patron, was repeatedly and unnecessarily asked by Bolduc to move out of the way. A refusal was finally given by Wooten. Werkowski's pool cue was then waved at Wooten and it was said by Werkowski that "You will be made to move by this." Werkowski's cue was taken from him by Wooten and laid down, and a proceeding was initiated in which Bolduc was shoved out of the door.

The glamour of science and technology is also responsible, we believe, for the vogue of certain words. "Utilize" is a good example. Lawyers who could never bring themselves to say "utilize" around the house—as in "Let's utilize your car tonight"—cannot bring themselves to write "use" in the office. They would feel stripped of their professional dignity if they were required to put "we used the coroner's telephone" on paper, instead of "we utilized the coroner's telephone." The allure of "utilize," we think, is not the subtle shade of meaning some lawyers attribute to it, but simply its scientific and technical air.

This section of a proposed settlement agreement in a federal sex discrimination case, regarding the obligation of an industry representative to recruit women, would have been backed by the court's contempt power:

> The Director shall develop a plan of action designed to maximize the Program's awareness and utilization of referral sources that can enhance the fulfillment of the purpose of this Decree.

Imagine the lawyers fighting over the meaning of this sentence in a contempt case for failing to perform.

"Utilize" is an easy device for making an ordinary phrase sound important. So is "type," as in "Some of the lamps had incandescent type bulbs"; and "process," as in "IP's size and complexity require an integrative management process"; and "impact" (used as a verb), as in "This research impacts corrections"; and "function" to refer to any entity for which the author has no better name, as in "The contract was negotiated by the company's wood procurement function in Mobile."

This last example, written by a corporate executive, also illustrates another mannerism of technical English that attorneys like to mimic: the use of nouns to modify other nouns, as in "wood procurement function." Readers encountering this structure have to readjust their interpretation of each word as it occurs. What appears at first to be a noun ("wood"), turns out to be an adjective, since it immediately precedes another noun ("procurement"), which subsequently also becomes an adjective, modifying yet another apparent noun (e.g., "function"). Thus an ambitious attorney can write about a wood procurement function or an offender records system and sound as authoritative as a NASA engineer. With a little practice, the attorney can generate strings of four or five consecutive nouns, all changing into adjectives, like caterpillars into butterflies, right before the reader's eyes: "We revised our estimate of the offender records system cost factor."

There is no grammatical rule to prevent children who survive their parents from being referred to as "children survivors"; or to prevent the distribution of their parents' estate from being called the "children survivor apportionment." For that matter, the principle upon which the apportionment was based could be called a "children survivor apportionment doctrine." And if the principle is expressed in a statute, that law might be said to have a "children survivor apportionment doctrine function," or even a "children survivor apportionment doctrine function capacity."

No grammatical rule prevents these constructions. After all, we often take ordinary nouns (e.g., "school" or "highway") and convert them into adjectives (e.g., "schoolteacher" or "highway patrol"). Why, then, do we find chains of technical nouns objectionable? We find them objectionable on aesthetic and practical grounds. Aesthetically, the noun chains we object to are ugly and pretentious —a subjective judgment, we admit, but one substantiated by the practice of writers published in the best magazines and journals for the educated public. Good writers rarely feel the need for strings of this sort, even when they are writing about technical subjects.

Practically speaking, a chain of nouns turning into adjectives places an unnecessary burden on the reader. Efficient reading can be defined as guessing what is about to appear next on the page and being right most of the time. Noun chains cause wrong guesses, requiring the reader to work forward and backward at the same time, anticipating what comes ahead and reinterpreting what has gone before. Moreover, noun chains appeal to lawyers because of their apparent efficiency. It takes fewer words to say "recipient benefit notification" than to say "notification of benefits available to the recipients." In such cases, we submit, more is better.

Despite the diversity of the symptoms, the underlying cause of bad legal writing can be reduced to a simple question of role playing. John and Joan mimic an artificial dialect that makes them sound like lawyers. They don the verbal equivalent of a three-piece suit and strut across the pages they write, thumb hooked in vest pocket, eyeglasses in the other hand, opining when they could be thinking, paying financial remuneration instead of money, and covering their traces with everything herein to the contrary notwithstanding.

The solution is simple. It is what Lord Balfour suggested: talk English, not law. It is, as Judge George Rose Smith implies, to back off for a moment and imagine how the matter would be expressed in a conversation at home. The structure and lexicon of spoken English is generally easier to comprehend than the relatively artificial structure and lexicon of writing. Lawyers are generally quite good at *talking* about the law. They can sit down with clients and explain obscure provisions in language a child could understand. It's only when they get next to a typewriter or a dictaphone that they lose their native grace with language. If only they would learn to talk on paper the way they talk in person when they choose to make themselves understood, most of their problems with language would disappear. If corporate lawyers were to follow this advice, credit contracts like the one we cited on page 4 might look like this:

> The seller may demand immediate payment in full if the buyer defaults on a payment, fails to maintain the insurance required by this contract, or fails to comply with any other provisions of this contract. The seller may also demand immediate payment in full if the seller has good reason to believe that the car is in danger of being misused or of being confiscated as payment of other debts the buyer may have incurred. If the buyer does not offer payment in full when asked to do so under any of these circumstances, the seller shall have all the rights provided by law, including the right to repossess the car and sell it again.

Insurance contracts like the one we cited on page 4 might read:

> A policyholder who is disabled during the grace period for payment of a premium and fails to pay it on time may still make a valid claim for total disability beginning during the grace period. The premium will have to be paid, however, with compound interest of 5 percent yearly, when proof of the claim is furnished to the company.

Law professors might be more enlightening if they avoided the dense prose we cited on page 5. What they meant to say, as best we can divine, was:

> The principle we tried to illustrate regarding the magnitude of a sentence is this: first decide a range of punishment suitable for all comparable offenders; then assign a punishment within that range, keeping in mind the need to deter others from committing the same offense.

And a divorce decree like the one cited on page 5 might come quickly and humanely to the point:

After hearing the evidence presented by both parties and their counsel, the Court has decided that this husband and wife are incompatible and that the plaintiff is entitled to the divorce she is seeking. Therefore, the marriage between them is hereby dissolved.

None of these revisions is memorable prose, but they are all more readable than their originals, and they all cover exactly the same legal ground as the originals. The main difference is that the revisions have a reasonably good chance of being understood by the people to whom they are addressed.

Whether John and Joan eventually serve their fellow citizens in storefront offices or from behind the bench of the U.S. Supreme Court, they would do well to accept the challenge of writing simply about complex matters. Then perhaps Senator William Proxmire would not have to give them his Golden Fleece Award, as he once gave the Supreme Court for writing: "Because a summary affirmance is an affirmance of the judgment only, the rationale of the affirmance may not be gleaned solely from the opinion below." Then, too, James J. Kilpatrick would not have to complain, as he once did after spending an afternoon reading a batch of opinions:

These birds are busy writing the supreme law of the land. They are dealing with the great gut issues of our country—racial tensions, sexual discrimination, employment, education, political, religious freedom, criminal trials. Yes, they must try to write precisely. But do they have to write precisely turgidly? Can't they write precisely lucidly instead?

When John and Joan become Esquires, they accomplish an impressive goal. If their training has been good, they have learned to think more analytically, more critically about human affairs than they did before going to law school. They have acquired new knowledge and a new language, much of it valuable, even essential for the tasks they will perform when they tack up their shingles. They have become part of a venerable tradition.

If their training has been typical, however, it has stopped short of applying critical habits of mind to one aspect of the legal tradition itself: the medium by which it is transmitted from generation to generation. Nobody in law school has asked them to analyze the language they use. No one has asked them to distinguish between terms of art and unnecessary jargon, between stylistic techniques that improve communication and stylistic mannerisms that impede it. No one has asked them to examine their language from the point of view of the nonlawyers who are expected to understand, abide by, and be protected by it.

This is what we are asking them to do now—to abandon their defenses, to examine the traditional verbiage and approach their style with the same critical rigor that they would bring to a new case or a new theory of law. If they do, John and Joan will be the prime beneficiaries, but the benefits will be shared by their clients, the public they serve.

2

Correctness: Reminiscing about the Future of the English Language

All legal writing is a battle against ambiguity, a battle that can never be entirely won. Words have multiple meanings. Sentences may be construed in more than one way. Clauses that seem fairly straightforward to a writer anticipating a given set of facts become nebulous to a reader trying to apply them to a novel situation. Eliminating these ambiguities is like plugging up the holes in a crumbling dike: each repair seems only to produce new leaks. Lawyers can define key terms in the preamble to a statute or contract, but their definitions are themselves expressed in words whose meaning can be misconstrued. Lawyers can add qualifications in anticipation of every conceivable set of circumstances, but the qualifications themselves may turn out to be sources of controversy.

Even though ambiguity can never be entirely removed from any text—there will always be readers somewhere who misinterpret what we write—some instances of ambiguity, like some errors in tennis, are more reprehensible than others because they should have been foreseen and avoided. Among the most inexcusable ambiguities in legal writing are those that occur when attorney-authors stray from what people generally perceive as correctness in written English: their punctuation, their grammar, or their use of words is at variance with the practice of established authors and professional editors. Whenever a lapse of this sort occurs, attorneys are in effect offering opposing counsel an opportunity to wiggle out of obligations that ought to have been clearly understood. They are requiring the courts to infer what their writing was supposed to have meant, when careful writers would have left no reasonable doubt about the meaning. And judges are, after all, only human. Given an opportunity to say what a statute, a rule, a clause in a will or contract *ought* to have meant, they will at times lean toward the interpretation closest to what they *wish* it meant. Bad grammar, in short, gives the courts not only the excuse but the obligation to become "activists" in their construction of the law.

When it comes to interpreting statutes, some courts seem to have given up hope in the possibility of grammatically accurate laws. A New Jersey Supreme Court judge, for example, had to interpret a provision of the state constitution pertaining to, of all things, the appointment of state judges.[1] Justice Jacobs quoted Learned Hand's remark that "there is no surer way to misread any document than to read it literally,"[2] and an 1859 New Jersey opinion holding that "Few statutes would stand if tried by standards of logic, grammar, or rhetoric."[3]

Other judges have reached the same conclusion, all but absolving legislators from any grammatical or lexical responsibility. "While the legislature is presumed familiar with the ordinary conventions of wording, punctuation and grammar, it is clear that many statutes are drafted with something short of perfection," wrote a federal court in New Jersey. That case involved a dispute between a motor carrier and the Interstate Commerce Commission over the words of a certificate authorizing the company's territorial limits.[4] Some judges even express disdain for the skills lawyers should have learned in elementary school. In a case involving the interpretation of a criminal charge of bribing a congressman, former U.S. Supreme Court Justice Felix Frankfurter wrote that "Statutes . . . are not inert exercises in literary composition. They are instruments of government, and in construing them 'the general purpose is a more important aid to the meaning than any rule which grammar or formal logic may lay down.' "[5] With a peculiar stylistic flair all his own, Frankfurter observed that "the purpose of an enactment is embedded in its words even though it is not always pedantically expressed in words." The Michigan Supreme Court in a case decided in 1873 shows a similar disdain for both grammar and logic: "Legislators are not grammar schools, and in this country, at least, it is hardly reasonable to expect legislative acts to be drawn with strict grammatical or logical accuracy."[6]

On the one hand, the attitude of these courts is refreshingly honest. As a matter of fact, many attorneys are incapable of policing their own grammar and usage, and to pretend otherwise would be delusory. On the other hand, as long as the courts assume that attorneys are incapable of expressing their intentions on paper, they take upon themselves the responsibility to determine what the document ought to have said, regardless of what the words on the paper seem to mean. Of course the courts will always have to use common sense to determine when the letter of a law is inconsistent with its obvious intent, but this is no excuse for ambiguities that could have been avoided by attention to the conventions of printed English.

Statutes (which are written by committees of lawyers and others) are not the only documents that can be disabled by sins against conventional usage: indictments, warrants, jury instructions, contracts, wills, and even ordinary letters can be torpedoed by simple editorial flaws. Each time this occurs, the balance of justice hangs on a wispy technicality. In one Illinois case an indictment was challenged because a singular noun, "a resident," was used in apposition to the names of two proposed defendants: "The said Wallace Hallberg and the said Howard Bengtson . . . not being a resident within the State of Illinois."[7] Whoever wrote the document had intended to indicate that both of the proposed defendants were nonresidents and thus were not beneficiaries of an exception to the statute of limitations. The accidental use of the singular "resident" gave Hallberg's attorney the opportunity to claim that the indictment was misleading. The Illinois Supreme Court agreed. "In the indictment before us," Justice Vickers wrote, "the word is used as a noun and is in the singular number. We are not aware of any rule of law that will authorize us to say that when the writer of an indictment uses a word which means one person he means two or more."[8] The indictment was dismissed.

In another case,[9] the Colorado Supreme Court dismissed a similar grammatical error as trivial and let a burglary conviction stand. It cited an earlier Colorado decision holding that language that would fail a composition test in school was acceptable in the courtroom.[10] "We may regret that those who write affidavits and warrants guard their pronouns with so little vigilance, but we cannot hold, as a matter of law, that their bad grammar vitiates the documents." The Colorado court decided that the defendants had been adequately advised of the charges against them despite the "legalistic and clumsy language" used in the charge.

Justice may have been done in this case as well as in the *Hallberg* case above; we do not dispute that. In both cases, however, judges were asked to make decisions that they would have not been asked to make if the attorneys had been more careful of their grammar. In each case the judge thought his ruling was based upon a decision about whether the defect would have misled the defendant and hampered the defense; but how are we to know that the real source of each judgment was not a predilection on the part of the judge, an inclination either to give defendants every conceivable benefit of doubt or to give that benefit to the prosecution?

Grammatical errors in jury instructions also cause kinks in due process that have to be unraveled at the discretion of the individual judge. One court ruled, for example, that obfuscatory language can invalidate a jury instruction. In an appeal that questioned the legality of an instruction on the meaning of reasonable doubt, Chief Judge Coffin held: "we cannot expect a jury to brush aside grammar and intuit a more sensible meaning, at least not when so crucial a concept as reasonable doubt is our focus."[11] An Ohio court decided that the grammar of an instruction on contributory negligence was consequential enough to have caused prejudicial error. In assessing the weight to be given to the words used by the trial judge in his instructions, the appeals court focused on the audience:

> Juries are composed of ordinary men on the street, not trained grammarians, and that fine distinction in the meaning of words and phrases are not ordinarily recognized by the average layman. Thus, in considering the propriety of any instruction, the meaning of the words used in the instruction must be thought of in their common meaning to the layman and not what such words mean to the grammarian or the trained legal mind.[12]

In all these cases, the judges may have ruled properly; but the attorneys, prosecutors, and judges themselves were at fault for committing the writing blunders that made these rulings necessary.

Legal writing in public documents—statutes, regulations, constitutions, and the like—can create profound problems of interpretation. The questions of meaning in these situations have raised classic jurisprudential debates that have tested the best minds and that never will be fully resolved. One traditional view is expressed in the frequently quoted statement of former Chief Justice Charles Evans Hughes that "a federal statute finally means what the Court says it means."[13] The other, the literalist or strict constructionist view, is typified by former Associate Justice Hugo Black's remarks about how he interpreted the meaning of the First Amendment:

> There are affirmative and negative words. The beginning of the First Amendment is that "Congress shall make no law." I understand that it is rather old-fashioned and shows a slight naivete to say that "no law" means no law. . . .[14]

> It is my belief that there are "absolutes" in our Bill of Rights, and that they were put there on purpose by men who knew what words meant, and meant their prohibitions to be "absolutes."[15]

As between private parties, the courts seem more inclined to hold authors responsible for their grammar, construing every ambiguity to the disadvantage of the writer. In a case involving charges of unfair labor practices based on a company rule banning union solicitations of workers on company time and premises, a federal court stated: "The true meaning of the rule might be the subject of grammatical controversy. However, the employees of respondent are not grammarians. The rule is at best ambiguous and the risk of ambiguity must be held against the promulgator of the rule rather than against the employees who are supposed to abide by it."[16]

A federal court in Iowa[17] was called upon to interpret the correct "syntax" of a sentence in an insurance policy. In question was the coverage of a company official killed while piloting a company plane. The provision of the company's policy was, in the court's words, "so befuddled that any number of meanings could be read into it." The insurance company intended to exclude coverage of aircraft owned or operated by the insured. It admitted the wording of its policy was confusing. The Court let the jury decide the meaning of the ambiguous provision. As a result, the insurance company was required to pay for the befuddling syntax of its attorneys.

In interpreting a provision of a lease, an Illinois district court first concluded that "the meaning of the words used here is obscure, and that the contract is therefore ambiguous," and then held: "Contracts are generally construed against the party who prepared them, for having chosen the words and grammar used, he is held responsible for the ambiguity."[18]

An experienced lawyer knows that cases of this sort could be multiplied without end. In general, attorneys who fail to mind their grammar give opposing counsel and unpredictable judges opportunities to ambush their intentions. Given the importance of precision in grammar and usage in the law, we have been dismayed to discover that the average attorney in our seminars is incapable of distinguishing subjects from predicates, much less dependent clauses from independent clauses. The distinction between restrictive and nonrestrictive modification—a distinction that can radically alter the punctuation and meaning of a sentence—is far beyond the ken of the average law school graduate.

Attorneys are not entirely to blame. Grammar has undergone a number of revolutions during the twentieth century, and as one judge put it, "the arbiters of grammar . . . themselves are not always in agreement and are aligned today in several schools of thought."[19] Justice O'Quinn of the Texas Court of Civil Appeals, reviewing a Texas statute governing the right of a pipeline company to install pipes in a railroad right of way, stated: "Any attempt by the courts to overrule the holdings of one school of grammarians and to sustain the pronouncements of another would be fruitless and a mere gratuity."[20]

Although ignorance of grammar is not confined to younger attorneys, they at least have the excuse that their English teachers may have taught them very little because they themselves were confused by the rapid succession of grammatical theories during the past several decades, culminating in the present state of affairs in which no single theory of grammar can be considered dominant. Even English professors are likely to know little or nothing about contemporary grammar, confounding it with rhetoric, linguistics, syntax, diction, lexicography, and punctuation, as if all of these words could be used interchangeably as synonyms for correctness.

In modern parlance, grammarians are people who study the structure of a language. (The structure of words is called morphology;

the structure of sentences is called syntax.) There are two major schools of grammarians: the prescriptive, or traditional, grammarians, who consider it their job to tell the world how the language *ought* properly to be used; and the descriptive, or scientific, grammarians, who hold that no one has the authority to say how a language ought to be used, and that the grammarian's job is to describe how a language *is* used. There are several competing theories within the scientific school of grammarians, but the distinctions between them are too technical for our purposes here.

Scientific grammarians are sometimes called linguists, a term that used to refer to persons who could speak several languages fluently, but is now used to describe people who study the structure of any language systematically. One of the main differences between linguists and traditional grammarians is their attitude toward the sort of language not ordinarily used in print. If traditional grammarians went to Southwest Louisiana, for example, where people might say, "Hey, cher, don't you eat no more of that boudin, no," they would no doubt be tempted to launch a linguistic pogrom against one of the most charming varieties of English on the face of the earth. If modern linguists heard the same sentence, they would simply take note of it, record it, analyze it, categorize it; but as scientists of language, they would no more pass judgment on it—positive or negative—than a botanist would pass judgment on a newly discovered herb.

Which school should attorneys hold with? Both. In their own writing, attorneys would do well to abide by the grammatical rules that other professional writers abide by because lapses from traditional grammar call attention to themselves, distracting the reader from the meaning of the text, sometimes even rendering that meaning impossible to construe. When they are construing what other people have written, however, attorneys need to be mindful that they cannot depend upon the person in the street or even the professional legal writer to abide by the rules preferred by traditional grammarians.

This in fact is what the courts seem to do, sometimes by instinct, sometimes by design. In a class action brought by consumers against Navy Commissaries for selling falsely labeled meat, a California court had to interpret the meaning of one provision of the State Consumer's Legal Remedies Act. It stated that in certain cases "the court shall permit the suit." In its holding, the court admitted that "justice is not the slave of grammar, and 'shall' has sometimes been judicially construed as directory or permissive."[21] There, however, the judge interpreted the language as mandatory because of the way it was used in the context of this particular statute's purposes.

In a case involving a tax loophole regarding collapsible corporations in a situation that never occurred to the drafters of the law, the court took a more balanced stand on grammatical conventions: "Courts are not captives of grammars and dictionaries. Neither are they free to ignore common usage and dictionary-tested meaning—especially in the field of tax legislation, where the necessities of the subject require technically exact language and certainty of meaning."[22]

An administrative law judge for the Federal Power Commission told us about one case that turned on his interpretation of the tenses of words used in a scientist's report about logging practices on a certain river. Here is how he dealt with the question in his opinion:

> He was, after all, obviously not reporting ancient events. He said logs "have been thrown . . . and floated," they "have been converted," the "rise of the water has commonly carried them safely" and their "passage over the falls has often been witnessed" (my emphasis). In good usage the present perfect tense does not denote an action that terminated in the distant past; correctly used, it refers to a just-completed or recently completed event, and we must assume that Dewey was familiar with proper usage. Therefore, even if he had not himself been an eyewitness, there would be less reason to question his report than if he had described a long-past occurrence.[23]

In our view, the judge's interpretation of the scientist's language was reasonable enough, but not necessarily for the grammatical reasons the judge gave. The scientist *did* happen to be using the present perfect tense in the way traditional grammarians say it ought to be used, and it is clear from the context that he meant what the judge said he meant. But what if the scientist, like many scientists, had spoken in a manner inconsistent with the traditional rules? Would the judge then have had to go by the book, even against the obvious sense as derived from context? We would say no; the courts, like grammarians and writers of dictionaries, have an obligation to look at the way language is actually used when they try to determine what its users are trying to say. People do not look in their grammar books before they open their mouths to speak. Or to borrow a phrase from a nineteenth-century grammarian quoted by a Texas judge, "All are free indeed from positive constraint in their phraseology; for we do not speak or write by statutes."[24]

Courts will rely on traditional grammar or ignore it when they consider it appropriate to do so. Whether we approve of this practice is irrelevant: it is the practice of the courts, and although mastery of traditional grammar may on occasion be ruled irrelevant to judicial proceedings, attorneys who have mastered it are, on balance, in a better position to wage their clients' battles than those who have not.

To attorneys who want to master the grammar they failed to learn as students, we can suggest a few inexpensive books that can be ordered in any bookstore. For general reference texts dealing with grammar and punctuation, there are a large number of college English handbooks on the market, most of which are competent and reliable. Two of the most popular are the *Harbrace College Handbook* (now in its eighth edition) and the *Prentice-Hall Handbook for Writers* (now in its seventh edition). The beauty of these books is their comprehensiveness: they contain definitions and examples of the most useful grammatical terms and the most frequent grammatical errors, and they give advice about spelling and punctuation, diction and style, vocabulary and usage, coherence and organization. They even have practice exercises at the end of many sections.

The weakness of these books, however, is that they are intended for classroom use, with the guidance of a teacher. They do not provide answers for the practice exercises, and sometimes in defining grammatical terms they use other grammatical terms a novice might not understand. Still, for lawyers who know at least a minimum of grammatical terminology, these books can come in handy.

Two of the more recent college texts on the market, *The Random House Handbook* by Frederick Crews and *Writing (Is an Unnatural Act)* by James C. Raymond (Harper and Row), include handbook sections that are less comprehensive than those mentioned above, but somewhat more accessible in style. They also include advice about style and organization in essay writing, which with minor adjustments for subject matter and audience would be useful to attorneys in composing legal documents of any kind.

For lawyers who would like to spend a few hours working through a do-it-yourself grammar text without the benefit of a teacher, we recommend *English 3200* by Joseph Blumenthal (Harcourt Brace Jovanovich). *English 3200* is a programmed text. It presents one bit of information at a time and then asks a question. The answer is given on the next page. If you answer the question correctly, you go on to the next bit of information; if you answer it incorrectly, you back up and reread the last bit of information until you understand why your answer was wrong. It is an ideal text for readers who want to teach themselves and are willing to devote some time to the task.

Many modern grammarians would view the texts we have recommended as very traditional, even reactionary. In recommending these texts for their practical value, we do not mean to suggest that modern grammarians are wandering off in useless explorations. On the contrary, modern grammarians have taught us a great deal about the way our language habits color and shape our perceptions of reality, about irrational biases that are implicit in the language we use and in our attitudes regarding the language other people use, and even about the nature of the human mind. When attorneys ask for grammar books, however, they are generally looking for information of a more practical sort.

One common grammatical problem in legal writing is the question of agreement, especially between pronouns and their antecedents. If a bank is involved in litigation, is it permissible to refer to the bank as "they"? This question arose in an interesting case that questioned a trial judge's instruction to a jury. The judge said that "they had set up this joint account between the husband and the wife and it's the contention that either one or both were liable to it under this account."[25] The bank claimed these words were ambiguous because the jury might conclude that the husband and wife set up the account rather than the bank.

The appellate court ruled that "the pronoun 'they' was intended by the trial court in its jury instructions . . . to refer to the noun 'bank.' " The appeals court said: "We think this usage by the trial court of the words mentioned was intended to convey such meaning, and we also believe that the use of words in this fashion is in keeping with the rule of English grammar applied in such cases."[26] We do not know where the judge found the rule: some traditional grammarians would no doubt quibble with it. Linguists, however, would agree with the judge: people do use plural pronouns to refer to businesses, as in "I prefer General Electric because they stand behind their products." In fact, the judge ruled on the basis of his own "close examination of the context in which it [the word *they*] was used" by the trial court in its instructions.

The problem becomes more perplexing if personal names are used as the name of a corporation. Should we refer to Wendy's as "it," "they," or possibly "she"? All three choices are awkward. Our advice is to avoid the problem by using some other designation altogether: usually, with a little ingenuity "the company" or "the corporation" can be used without ambiguity in context, and referred to as "it" in subsequent references. Sometimes it is possible to identify the actual persons involved in a discussion and to use them as referents: thus instead of using "the bank," and wondering whether it should be followed by "it" or "they," the judge in the Tuscaloosa case might have used "the teller" or "the loan officer" or whoever it was, and followed it by "he" or "she" as appropriate.

But not, we hope, by "he/she." While we are perfectly sympathetic with feminist sensibilities in the matter of pronoun choice, we find that in almost every case we can respect these sensibilities without mutilating the language or inventing new words. For example, when the situation calls for the use of nouns in a generic sense, as in "Attorney for the defense should file his or her brief with the clerk," the easiest solution is to avoid the problem by using plurals: "Attorneys for the defense should file their briefs with the clerk." In ordinary usage, the plural in this context includes the singular, so that no one could reasonably infer from a sentence like this that a defendant was obliged to have more than one attorney, or that an attorney was obliged to have more than one brief (any more than it could be inferred from the singular version that a defendant is limited to one attorney with one brief).

One traditional way to solve the problem has been to place a disclaimer on the end of the document, like this one we found at the end of a will written by one of the largest and most prestigious firms in Washington, D.C.:

> Throughout this Will, the masculine and neuter genders shall be deemed to include all genders, or the singular the plural and vice versa, except where such construction would be unreasonable.

The effect, obviously, is not to clarify any ambiguity in the pronoun references, but simply to give the heirs permission to wrestle with whatever problems may arise. For that they didn't need to pay an attorney.

We also reviewed a partnership agreement in which one of the partners insisted on "his/her" instructions to protect the gender of both partners. The performance clause reads:

> Each partner will apply all of his/her experience, training, and ability to the performance of the work of the partnership, and to the furthering of the business interest of the partnership.

And the withdrawal clause reads:

> Any partner may withdraw from the partnership for any reason. In this circumstance, the withdrawing partner shall give the remaining partners notice at the earliest possible time of his/her impending departure.

One possible solution would have been to use the colloquial idiom in which plural pronouns are used to refer to singular but indefinite antecedents, as in "Everyone enjoyed themselves at the party." Another would have been to avoid the problem by using plurals ("Both partners will employ their experience . . .") or to recast the wording entirely ("The partner who decides to withdraw will announce the intended date of departure to the other partner as soon as possible"). This is a fine point, of course. Our position is that sex-neutral language is best if it doesn't call attention to itself. If the parties involved prefer the more explicit his/her references, however, for their symbolic value—well, maybe the aesthetics of style ought occasionally to take a backseat to other reasonable sensibilities.

Some critics of sexism in language have gone so far as to criticize such words as conman (conperson?), and person (perdaughter?), and helium (shelium?). Legal draftsmen should heighten their consciousness to claims of sexism in legal writing, but they should not twist language into awkward and artificial words that produce laughter rather than enlightenment.[27]

Another common grammatical problem for attorneys is the dangling or misplaced modifier. The classic classroom example of this offense is "Driving down Main Street, an elephant appeared in my rearview mirror." Obviously the writer did not mean to suggest that the elephant was driving down Main Street, but that literally is the meaning of the sentence. Initial modifiers (in this case the participle, "driving") normally modify the grammatical subject of the sentence (in this case, "elephant").

The most frequent offenders in this regard are judges who close their opinions with something like "Based on the foregoing arguments and evidence, the Court hereby rules that . . ." The sentence literally means that the *Court* is based on the foregoing arguments and evidence, which of course is not what the judge intends to say. The judge intends to say that the *ruling* is based on those considerations, but his syntax, or hers, has jumped its tracks.

The error is harmless enough in this instance, but it sometimes results in comic disruptions. In an industrial safety case, for example, we once read that "Complainant's inspector standing approximately a hundred feet away testified that the load line came within three or four feet of the power line." We can imagine the courtroom scene: the judge behind his bench, the complainant's inspector a hundred feet away delivering his testimony from the back of the courtroom.

Our favorite example of the misplaced modifier comes from a Kansas opinion in which prison officials seem to have been blamed for the very offenses they were trying to correct: "Following alleged coercive participation in certain sexual acts the prison administration granted his request to be placed in the Adjustment and Treatment Building under protective custody." Prison conditions have reached an all-time low if even the administration behaves that way!

Another problem for lawyers is the temptation to use "and/or" and "either/or." Although we have no grammatical quarrel with these phrases, they do seem to call attention to themselves because we never see them used in the best journalistic writing, even when that writing is quite technical and precise. In one case, a Texas judge went so far as to declare *and/or* "meaningless," an "abominable invention . . . as devoid of meaning as it is incapable of classification by the rules of grammar and syntax."[28] The case concerned a workmen's compensation claim by a widow and children who claimed the deceased died of a heatstroke on the job doing road construction. The complaint said the cause of death was heat prostration and/or drinking foul water. Heatstroke was proved; the other claim was not. The question was whether the use of the words "and/or" required independent proof of both claims.

To solve this problem, we need to understand first why it is a problem. The culprit is the English word *or*. In some languages there is more than one word for *or*. In Latin, for example, *aut* means "one or the other, but not both," while *vel* means "one or the other and possibly both." English has no such luxury. The English word *or* might be translated into Latin either as *aut* or *vel*, depending upon the writer's intention. The attorney's use of "and/or," therefore, is an intuitive attempt to remedy this deficiency in English. Unfortunately, the remedy does not work. When a contract says that royalties are to be paid "to the author and/or to his heirs," it is not at all clear who must be paid in order to satisfy the conditions of the contract.

We also object to "and/or" on aesthetic grounds. Because the best journalists and writers seem able to say exactly what they mean without recourse to "and/or," we suspect that attorneys could do so as well if they chose to do so. It might cost them a few extra words, but in this situation we would consider the extra words well spent. If, for example, an insurance company was agreeing to pay for any damages that might be caused to a "boat and/or its outboard motor," the contract might just as well read "either to the boat, or to its motor, or to both." If the company wanted to pay for one sort of damage but not the other, it might write "either to the boat or to its motor, but not to both." These expanded phrases not only seem more graceful, but they also require the writer to think about what the insurance company wants to cover and to express that coverage as precisely as possible.

In some cases, the boundaries between grammar, usage, and lexicography seem to dissolve in a dispute about what a given word or phrase really means. Philosophically, of course, there is no absolute answer to this question, no more than there is an absolute answer to "How far is Mars?" The answer depends upon where and when you ask the question, and even then only an approximate and obsolescent answer is possible. Words and phrases do not have absolute meanings, independent of subjective human audiences and immune from the changes that time wreaks on all things mortal. The key question is not what does the word mean, but what does it mean to the persons who were supposed to have understood and abided by it.

For example, we reviewed a disputed lease in which there was a renewal clause at the tenant's option at a monthly rate that the lessor could raise "to 105 percent of the amount of the last month's rent." When the lease came up for renewal, the landlord wanted to double the rent, and then add 5 percent; the tenant argued that, according to the contract, the rent could be raised by 5 percent, not by 105 percent. Who was right? What did the clause *really* mean? Obviously it meant one thing to the lessor and another to the tenant. Dictionaries were not much help, because small words, like "to," are typically given two or three columns of definitions rather than a single pronouncement that would settle the dispute. The tenant did what the courts themselves normally do: they ask experts—in this situation, an English professor, a professor of contract law, and a real estate broker—what the disputed clause meant to them. The experts in this case agreed that if the lessor had meant to reserve the right to raise the rent *by* 105 percent, then the lease should have used the word *by*, and there would have been no ambiguity. But raising it *to* 105 percent meant a 5 percent raise, and that was all the happy tenant had to pay.

In cases like this one, the opinion of a professional grammarian or lexicographer is sometimes inconsequential. What matters is what the words would have meant to the readers for whom they were intended. A subjective judgment? Of course. But the meaning of all words is nothing more than a confluence of subjective judgments. The issue is simply *whose* subjective judgment matters in a given case. In a libel case based on an employer's letter to its customers stating that the plaintiffs, former employees, "have been terminated,"[29] the judge ruled that it made no difference what grammarians might have said about the meaning of the libelous phrase. The plaintiffs understood the phrase to mean that they had been fired, and so did a number of other lay witnesses "who did not profess to be grammarians." "The meaning the average reader would give the letter was not a question for the opinions of grammarians," the court held. If the authors of the phrase had intended some other meaning, they should have used other words.

Another case, a divorce trial in Alabama, was suddenly turned around when a witness, quite properly, demanded a definition of terms. The issue was whether the husband had committed adultery. The wife's lawyer asked a woman witness whether she had had sexual relations with the husband. She replied that she had. After her testimony was completed and as she was leaving the courtroom, she stopped, turned and asked the judge: "Did he mean to ask whether I had intercourse with this guy?" When the judge replied that this indeed was the purpose of the question, she returned to the witness stand and testified that she never had "intercourse" with the respondent, only "sexual relations." The euphemism used by the attorney obviously covered, in her mind at least, forms of dalliance that are not grounds for divorce.

Strictly speaking, it is the business of lexicographers (dictionary writers) to watch over the meaning of words. And, strictly speaking, it is the business of lexicographers to describe language, not to invent it. But there have always been choices to make, choices that inevitably reflect assumptions and value judgments on the part of the lexicographer. In the eighteenth century, when Dr. Samuel Johnson wrote the first great English dictionary, there were (as there still are today) a number of dialects of English spoken in Great Britain. Since it would have been impossible to record the language in its entirety with all the variations peculiar to different geographical regions or socioeconomic classes, Dr. Johnson instinctively chose the variety of English that sounded most "proper" to his ears—namely the sort of English that was used in speech and in writing by people like him, educated people whose language was no barrier to acceptance in the most prestigious social circles. As it turned out, however, Dr. Johnson's dictionary, like most dictionaries after it, was popularly perceived not as a description of the language preferred by a literary elite, but as a description of the way English ought to be spoken by people who would like to speak it "correctly."

When lexicographers decide what a word really means, they have two choices: they can examine the history of the word and decide what it ought to mean on the basis of what it used to mean; or they can collect samples of sentences in which the word is used and infer from context what the word currently seems to mean to people who use it.

As an example of the first method, some authorities are opposed to the use of the word "convince" followed by "to," as in "We convinced the court to grant a delay." Why? Because, say these experts, "convince" comes from the Latin *convincere*, meaning to bind down in chains, and it makes little sense to get people to do things or go places by binding them in chains. "Persuade," according to this school of thought, would work better in this sentence. "Convince" would be acceptable in a sentence like "We convinced the court that our client was innocent," because no motion or action follows the verb.

Taken to its extreme, this approach to lexicography would mean that no one could properly use the language without knowing the history of every word. And even then it would be difficult to decide how far back in history we should travel before deciding that we had discovered a "true" meaning.

Meaning is not the only aspect of language that changes: usage, which is the way we treat words grammatically, changes as well. One example is the way we form the plural of a word like "formula." Anyone who has had high school Latin knows that the Romans formed the plural by adding an *e* to the singular, making it *formulae*—and that is exactly how the plural was formed in English too, when more people studied Latin. Now, however, *formula* has become Anglicized, so that the preferred plural, in many dictionaries, is *formulas*, and *formulae* seems somewhat pedantic.

As if changes in meaning and syntax were not enough to contend with, lexicographers have to study new words that are invented to name new inventions, new fashions, new procedures. Often these new words are constructed on some logical basis.

Lawyers, for example, often speak of Shepherdizing cases—a term that means nothing to nonlawyers, even those who make dictionaries. The word comes from the proper name Shepherd, Inc., a firm in Colorado Springs that compiles periodic indexes to published decisions so attorneys can conveniently discover whether a point of law established in any given case has been affected by more recent court rulings. To Shepherdize, therefore, means to research a case using Shepherd's citation indexes.

As far as we know, however, there is no widely accepted term for the new surgical procedures by which people have their sexes changed. Whoever invents the term we hope will be more sensitive to language than the attorney who, in representing an airline pilot who had a sex change operation, referred to it as a "gender re-assignment."

Because of the problems inherent in trying to capture language and prevent it from changing, modern lexicographers have generally given up on the notion that they should act as arbiters of propriety. Instead, they collect samples of a given word used at a given time and infer from context what the word means and how it is treated grammatically. *Webster's New Collegiate Dictionary*, for example, illustrates the meaning of "convince" with the phrase "*convinced* them to leave the country," a usage that would be as welcome to the ears of traditional grammarians as the sound of chalk squeaking on the blackboard. *Webster's* underlying philosophy, however, is that words change meaning continuously, and the responsibility of lexicographers, like the responsibility of scientists in any field, is to report what they observe, not what they wish they had observed.

Even though most lexicographers gather samples and make inferences from them, there is still considerable diversity among dictionaries. All lexicographers agree that words ought to be defined by inference from samples of their actual use. They argue heatedly, however, over just whose usage should be included in the sample. In *Webster's Third New International Dictionary*,[30] the editors decided that spoken English was as important a source as written English, and therefore illustrated its definitions with lines attributed to people like Willie Mays, Dwight Eisenhower, Ethel Merman, Jimmy Durante, and others who are highly esteemed by the general public, but not for the quality of their writing. It also cites printed sources using words in ways that would offend traditional grammarians; *Webster's* seems to suggest, however, that what is done in prestigious journals, like the *Harvard Business Review*, indicates the actual state of current usage better than any grammatical prescription.

For years, *Webster's Third* was something of *cause célèbre* in editorial circles. It was attacked furiously by writers and editors who wanted dictionaries to give them guidance about how to use the language properly. Suddenly the second edition of *Webster's New International Dictionary* became a prestige item, when it was supposed to have become supplanted by the newer edition.

Partly as a reaction to *Webster's Third*, the *American Heritage*

Dictionary was published in 1969. In determining meaning and proper usage, the editors of the *American Heritage* also collected samples, but they were very particular about the sources of their samples. Whenever they came to a word with disputed usage, the editors consulted a panel that consisted mainly of people who are in one way or another professionally associated with writing or editing. Thus the advice and definitions in the *American Heritage* often reflect the opinions of a relatively small group of people who are likely to view words from a writer's perspective.

A good way to compare dictionaries is to take a troublesome word and see how various dictionaries treat it. *Data* is a good example. In Latin, *data* is a plural form, but in English it strikes many people as collective and therefore singular. Should we say "these data have no significance" or "this data has no significance"?

Webster's Third, typically, does not indicate a preferred usage; it simply says that data is plural, but "often" singular in construction, citing an example from *Publisher's Weekly* in which data is treated as singular: "until more data is available." The *American Heritage* is a little more explicit in its advice, saying that "data is now used both as a plural and as a singular," giving examples apparently contrived by the editors themselves, and adding that "the singular is acceptable to 50 percent of the Usage Panel." Somewhere between *Webster's Third* and the *American Heritage* in philosophy is *The Random House Dictionary*, published in 1966. It says that data is "usually construed as singular," adding one example using the word in the singular, another using it in the plural. *Data* obviously is a word in the midst of a grammatical shift. The conservative choice is to treat it as plural (these data have . . .), but in all likelihood *data* will soon follow the path of *opera* and *agenda,* both plural forms in Latin, but resolutely singular in English.

Which dictionary should attorneys have? All of them, if possible. Each dictionary has its own purpose. When attorneys want guidance about how they themselves ought to use a particular word, we recommend the *American Heritage,* because it is likely to indicate the most conservative usage, which is the easiest usage to defend if the document is ever questioned in court. When they want to know what a word means to the general public or how it is treated grammatically by ordinary nonwriters, attorneys would do better to consult *Webster's Third. Webster's* would be the more appropriate source to consult, for example, in determining what a testator might have meant in a will he wrote, or what an insured party might reasonably have understood by a disputed word in a policy, or what a witness meant by a statement that might be anathema to editors but ordinary usage by ordinary people.

The only people who have absolute authority to assign meanings to words are those who create new gadgets and then decide what to name them. That, as one federal court held in a patent dispute over an apparatus for casting screws, is what the courts mean when they say that "a patentee may be his own lexicographer and, we add, his own grammarian."[31] Even this authority has its limits, however. As the court pointed out, in conveying his thoughts through language, the patentee must "do so in such a way that his counsel cannot give a different meaning to his words before the Patent Office than he does before the courts."[32]

Legislators, too, have the authority to fix meanings, as they often do in the beginning of statutes, where they say how various words are to be construed. And in fact attorneys may define words as they please in drafting wills, contracts, and other agreements. For example, a clause we recently reviewed in a publishing contract reads: "For the purpose of this contract, the word 'author' refers to the author and any revising authors." Another version of this kind of definition appeared in a clause stating that in this contract, "The work includes Volume 1, but not the accompanying synopsis, which will be governed by a separate agreement."

The variability of language—the fact that any one language is spoken somewhat differently by each of its individual speakers and the fact that any one language as a whole is changed with the passage of time—is a source of some consternation in our culture today. If, as the linguists tell us, all varieties of English are inherently equal, then what right do schoolteachers have to discriminate between correct and incorrect usage? If all the varieties are equal, then shouldn't students have a right to use the variety they bring with them to school, the variety spoken by their families at home?

If, on the other hand, we surrender completely to change and variety in language, how will we ever express ourselves in words others can rely on? What sort of civilization would be possible if we conceded to the linguists and critics who say that because language is an arbitrary symbol system, and because no two people possess the same amount of any language or possess it in exactly the same way, there is no intrinsically "correct" interpretation for anything we write or say? If that is the case, how can we fashion the laws, contracts, and agreements we need to make social behavior orderly and just?

Oddly enough, there is no logical middle ground between these two points of view. The linguists are in fact correct: language is arbitrary and unstable. Yet there is another side of language, a side not entirely tractable with the inductive methods used by linguists. This other side might be called the phenomenology of language: the unshakable conviction we all have that we are making sense to one another in our conversations, that we are understanding the same messages when we listen to a newscaster on TV, that we get the same information when we each read the morning paper on our own. Linguists may tell us that this conviction of ours is an illusion, but at least it's an illusion we can count on.

Because language is the medium of their trade, attorneys have no choice but to come to grips intellectually with the nature of language, to understand the facts of change, but to be reasonably well informed about the way words are used by other people whose business it is to use them carefully. Linguists may point out that even Shakespeare used "infer" when later usage experts would have preferred "imply," but that would be no excuse for an attorney today to ignore the distinction educated people draw between those two words, however arbitrary that distinction may be.

Attorneys cannot afford to be as careless as the expert witness who described herself as a "prolific reader." "Prolific," from the Latin word meaning offspring, suggests a productive role, not a passive one. The expert was no doubt a voracious reader, though one would suspect not a very careful one.

Nor can attorneys afford to be as careless as the personal injury lawyer who described his client as "limping profusely." "Profuse" comes from a Latin word meaning "to pour out"; to use that word properly the lawyer should have found himself a client who was bleeding. People can limp profusely and read prolifically only if these words have been reduced to mean nothing more than "a lot," so that it would make just as much sense to read profusely and limp prolifically.

And then we will have good reason to reminisce about the future of the English language, though not without some grave misgivings.

3

Punctuation Who Can Hang by a Comma?

In most businesses and professions, punctuation may be regarded as a trivial matter—a clerical skill that can be entrusted to secretaries and copy editors. In law, however, cases involving huge sums of money and even human lives hang on the interpretation of a single comma or semicolon. Lawyers who depend upon their clerical staffs to put in the proper marks might just as well ask their typists to draft the contracts and briefs themselves.

In law, punctuation makes meaning. Legal documents are interpreted on the basis of editorial conventions that most lawyers seem to understand only vaguely, if at all.

In 1976, to avoid the expense of a special election, the state of Alabama attempted to conduct a referendum on a constitutional amendment along with the regularly scheduled general election. But the constitution in Alabama requires that elections on proposed amendments take place at the first general election after the legislative session in which they are proposed or "upon another date appointed by the legislature, not less than three months after the final session of the legislature. . . ."[1] As it happened, the general election was to take place just less than ninety days after the legislature had adjourned. The comma before "not less than" in this passage suddenly became the subject of intense debate in Alabama. Had that comma been omitted, officials finally decided, the legislature would have been free to put the amendment on the general election ballot and save the state half a million dollars in costs for a special election.

The Kentucky Court of Appeals had to construe a will to decide whether an estate was to be divided into nine equal parts, or into eight parts with one part shared by two parties.[2] The key passage was this one, in which the semicolons seem to mark clear boundaries between eight sets of beneficiaries:

> I bequeath and devise my entire estate, both personal and real, which may remain after the satisfaction of the above special bequest and the payment of my debts, funeral expenses, and the costs and expenses of the administration of my estate, *in equal shares, absolutely and in fee to my cousin, the said Walter Cassidy; Robert Jamison and William Stivers, tenants on my farm; George E. Smith, who rents my property on Bland Avenue, Shelbyville, Kentucky; and the Kentucky Society for Crippled Children, of Louisville, Kentucky; Baptist Ministers Aid Society, of Owensboro, Kentucky; Baptist Orphan's Home of Louisville, Kentucky; King's Daughters' Hospital, of Shelbyville, Kentucky; and the Clayvillage Baptist Church, of Clayville, Shelby County, Kentucky* [emphasis added].

Was it editorial craftsmanship or simple negligence that caused the attorney who drafted this will to join two separate beneficiaries with a conjunction, while all the rest were separated by semicolons? Was it sheer guesswork or a sure knowledge of the rules that guided the Court in deciding that Jamison and Stivers should each have one-ninth of the bequest, instead of sharing one-eighth?

The Kentucky Court of Appeals disagreed with the contention that Jamison and Stivers must share one-eighth of the estate because, it was argued, "The semicolon after the names of Jamison and Stivers and its omission between their names, illustrates that such was the testator's intention." The appellate court decided instead that "the testator divided the residue of his estate into nine equal shares."

The Court disregarded the conventions of punctuation and followed its own judicial rule for the construction of wills. In deciding the testator's intention, the Court held, it would "look to the language used in the will. If in so doing his intention can be ascertained, and it is not contrary to public policy, that intention controls, regardless of collateral and subsidiary rules which may be employed in arriving at the intention when it is obscure."

The Court preferred equality of inheritance to correctness in punctuation. Only the deceased knows if this was a correct ruling.

The Supreme Judicial Court of Maine went so far as to declare itself emancipated from the ordinary rules of punctuation in construing the meaning of its state's extradition statute.[3] The law in question provided that another state's demand for a fugitive "shall be accompanied by *a copy of an indictment found, or information, supported by an affidavit . . .*" (emphasis added).

The question was whether the New York indictment presented to the Maine court by New York authorities had to be supported by an affidavit. The use of the commas in the italicized part of the statute certainly requires that conclusion. But the Maine judges did not conclude so. They said the commas "merely reflect an approach to punctuation by Maine's legislative draftsmen different in form, but not in substance, from that of the uniform laws commissioners' committee on style." And everyone else's, it might be added.

Dropping both commas or at least the second comma would make the sentence in question say what the Maine court said it said. But the Court was interested in "justice" and ruled that in view of the clear legislative history of this law and of the need for consistency between states in these kinds of cases, it would rewrite the poorly punctuated sentence.

The Court acknowledged that "punctuation can help in construing an unclear statute," but found that the commas in this case "are themselves the sole cause of any ambiguity at all in that section." The Court ignored the possibility that the state's legislative draftsmen wrote what they meant to write.

A colleague of ours whose law practice centers on sex and race discrimination cases showed us a statute[4] whose meaning was twisted because of a missing comma. In researching a Title VII issue, he read the following sentence concerning a party's right to intervene in a lawsuit brought by the government: "the person or persons aggrieved shall have the right to intervene in a civil action brought by the Commission or the Attorney General in a case involving a government" §706(F)(1).

This sentence appears to say that an aggrieved person has the right to intervene only in cases brought against a government.

Actually, an aggrieved person can intervene in *any* case brought by the commission, as well as in cases brought by the attorney general against a government. This is clear only if you struggle through a page-long paragraph. The quoted sentence would have the correct meaning if Congress had punctuated it properly, by putting a comma after "Commission" and by adding the word "by" after the word "or."

Punctuation in legal documents can indeed be a matter of life and death. In Maryland, the interpretation of the capital punishment statute hinged on the significance of one comma.[5] The defendant in this case had been convicted of murder, second-degree rape, and illegal use of a gun. The question concerned the possible sentence. Capital punishment was authorized by law if "the defendant committed the murder while committing or attempting to commit robbery, arson, *or rape or sexual offense in the first degree*" (emphasis added).

There was no legislative history to tell the judge whether the Maryland legislature intended to require only the sexual offense or both the sexual offense and the rape to be in the first degree. With no authoritative legal explanation of the meaning of the law, the judge went to his grammar books and decided that the modifying words "in the first degree" must be read to apply to both of the offenses following the last comma. The defendant's life was saved by the judge's good grammar. We don't pretend that punctuation always involves stakes as high as these, but punctuation obviously is no mere cosmetic in legal writing.

Lawyers have another reason for learning to punctuate. The legal profession is inescapably a literate one. Attorneys can rely only so far on oral arguments, telephone calls, contacts, and conferences to get their business done. Sooner or later every important transaction is nailed down in writing—a brief, a will, a contract, a settlement, a regulation, a statute. Lawyers instinctively advise their clients to "get it in writing"; virtually every suit is settled on an interpretation of something that has been written by someone somewhere. Because written documents are the very stuff of their trade, good lawyers and good judges are fastidious about the details of editorial conventions. Good lawyers know the rules. When they see careless violations of the conventions, they wince. Improper punctuation, even when it does not obscure meaning, is regarded as a sign of intellectual sloppiness. It undermines the authority of the writer.

When we say good lawyers know the rules, we may be overstating our case. What most lawyers—even the good ones—don't know is that there is no single set of rules. The "rules" of punctuation aren't really rules at all. They are conventions, habits, traditions that readers expect to see honored in print simply because they have become accustomed to them. These conventions have been in a state of continuous evolution since English was first put on paper in the Middle Ages. There has never been universal agreement about punctuation, and even editors in the best publishing houses will argue about the "correct" punctuation of an unusual sentence.

British lawyers seem to have put disagreements of this sort to rest. With their characteristic disdain for the superfluous, they make do without any punctuation at all. Ralph G. Holberg, Jr., an attorney in Mobile, sent us the following example—a passage from an agreement between a British firm and an American firm.

PRICING
8. (1) Subject as hereinafter mentioned Smythe agrees to purchase at Prices (as defined in Clause 1) Products from Jones and Jones agrees to sell at such Prices the Products to Smythe
(2) The Prices are subject to alteration by Jones before shipment ex works (provided that such alterations are applicable to Jones's prices to its other distributors and dealers) in which event Smythe may either :—
(a) accept the Products at the altered price
   or
(b) cancel the order within fourteen days of service of notice of alteration   If the order is not cancelled within the specified time Smythe shall be deemed to have accepted the Products at the altered price

The names have been changed, but the document is otherwise authentic. The passage, Mr. Holberg assures us, is typical of the entire eleven-page contract. It is generous in its use of parentheses, overly generous in its use of capital letters, and inventive in its use of a colon followed by a dash. But there are no commas anywhere, and no periods—not even after the sentences that end at 8(1) and within section 8(2)(b). When the American attorneys wondered whether shortages in Britain had begun to affect the supply of punctuation marks, the British assured them that "legal draftsmanship in England was accomplished without punctuation quite deliberately and in the interest of clarity in the document itself."

We do not say that the British contract is improperly punctuated. It is properly punctuated according to a tradition that bears scarcely any resemblance to ordinary editorial conventions on either side of the Atlantic.

Lawyers in the United States do not enjoy this sort of editorial independence. They are expected to conform to the same conventions that the better commercial and academic publishing houses follow. They are expected to use commas and periods just as other literate people use them.

If the British have managed to write clear documents with sparse punctuation, Americans seem adept at writing obscure documents with abundant punctuation. The following passage is the regulation governing the use of the law library in the District of Columbia jail. As you read it, imagine that you are a typical inmate, wondering whether you can use the library tomorrow afternoon.

GENERAL ORDER: USE OF THE LAW LIBRARY

WITH THE EXCEPTION OF ALTERNATE THURSDAYS, THE FIRST MONDAY OF THE MONTH, AND ANY WEEKS IN WHICH A NATIONAL OR STATE HOLIDAY IS CELEBRATED ON A WEEKDAY, INMATES ARE ONLY PERMITTED TO USE THE LAW LIBRARY ("USE" BEING DEFINED AS BEING PRESENT IN THE LAW LIBRARY AND READING LAWBOOKS—THE ONLY USE OF THE FACILITY THAT IS PERMITTED, LOITERING BEING SPECIFICALLY FORBIDDEN AND NOT PERMITTED FOR ANY REASON WHATSOEVER) ON MONDAYS AND TUESDAYS BETWEEN THE HOURS OF 9 O'CLOCK A.M., AND 12 NOON, 6 O'CLOCK P.M., AND 9 O'CLOCK P.M., WEDNESDAYS, BETWEEN THE HOURS OF 2 O'CLOCK P.M., AND 5:30 O'CLOCK P.M., THURSDAYS, AFTER SECOND ROLL CALL CLEARS (UNLESS IT CLEARS AFTER 12 NOON, IN WHICH CASE TUESDAY'S SCHEDULE APPLIES), AND 5 O'CLOCK P.M., FRIDAYS, AFTER 4 O'CLOCK P.M., AND 9 O'CLOCK P.M., AND SATURDAYS, BETWEEN 7 O'CLOCK P.M., AND 9 O'CLOCK P.M.

Ironically, the motive behind this sort of writing is clarity. Lawyers fear periods. They worry that qualifications may be ignored if they are added beyond the boundary of a sentence. They think that in order to achieve clear understandings, they must stuff every related idea into a single sentence between an initial capital letter and a final period.

They are, of course, wrong. The library regulations would be both clearer and more defensible in a lawsuit if they were expressed in a few short sentences.

The first rule of punctuation lawyers need to learn is simple.

RULE 1: Do not fear periods. Use them often, especially to break up long, awkward sentences.
EXAMPLE:
The D.C. jail notice could have been written this way, for example:

Inmates may use the law library at the following times:

Monday	9 A.M.–12; 6 P.M.–9 P.M.
Tuesday	9 A.M.–12; 6 P.M.–9 P.M.
Wednesday	2 P.M.–5:30 P.M.
Thursday	After the second roll call clears (if it clears after noon, follow Tuesday's schedule) until 5 P.M.
Friday	4 P.M.–9 P.M.
Saturday	7 P.M.–9 P.M.

The library will be closed on the following days:
1. alternate Thursdays.
2. the first Monday of each month.
3. national or state holidays falling on a weekday.

The library may be used solely to read lawbooks. Loitering is prohibited.

Besides this rule, there are nine others every lawyer should thoroughly understand. Professional editors naturally apply many more rules; we have chosen to give only those that lawyers and judges ask us about most frequently. Situations not covered by our list are likely to be treated in stylebooks, some of which are described at the end of this chapter.

RULE 2: Put a comma before *and* between the last two items in a series of three or more.
EXAMPLE:
The parking lot attendant noticed a stocking, a pistol, and a bundle of cash on the front seat of the car.

There are two schools of thought regarding the comma before *and* in a series. In our opinion, the weight of authority in favor of the comma is greater: it is recommended by all of the stylebooks discussed at the end of this chapter. For dissenting opinions, see the *Associated Press Stylebook* and the *United Press International Stylebook.*

RULE 3: Use a pair of commas to set off material that adds information without affecting the meaning of the rest of the sentence.
EXAMPLE:
Our first case, *Walton* v. *Smith Jewelry,* is now on appeal.

Grammarians would call "*Walton* v. *Smith Jewelry*" a nonrestrictive modifier in this example. Nonrestrictive means nonessential. The meaning of the sentence would not change if "*Walton* v. *Smith Jewelry*" was omitted: "Our first case is now on appeal." Because the writers can have had only one first case, the name of the case is interesting, but not essential to the meaning of the sentence.

In applying this rule, take care not to put commas around information that provides essential identification.

EXAMPLE:
Attorneys, who are required to take CLE courses, may claim as deductions all costs incurred in connection with this seminar.

The commas in this sentence indicate that the meaning of the sentence would not be materially affected by the omission of the words between the commas: "Attorneys may claim as deductions all costs incurred in connection with this seminar." Obviously this is not the intended meaning. *Only* those attorneys who are required to take CLE courses may claim the deduction. To express this restriction, the commas should be omitted: "Attorneys who are required to take CLE courses may claim as deductions. . . ." Grammarians would call "who are required to take CLE courses" a restrictive modifier. Restrictive modifiers have the force of *only*; they limit (restrict) the term they modify.

RULE 4: Put a comma before a coordinate conjunction joining independent clauses.
EXAMPLE:
The store had refunded the complainant's money, and the complainant had returned the faulty appliances.

The secret to identifying coordinate conjunctions is to memorize them. There are only five of any consequence: *and, but, or, nor,* and *for*.

An independent clause is simply a group of words that will make sense by itself as a sentence. For example, "The store had refunded the complainant's money" is an independent clause. It makes sense as a sentence in itself. So does "The complainant had returned the faulty appliances."

There is one exception to the rule: the comma may be omitted if the independent clauses are very short.

EXAMPLE:
The judge pronounced the sentence and the defendant's fate was sealed.

How short is short? This is a judgment call, not worth much agony. As a rule of thumb, if the independent clauses are five words or less, the comma before *and* may be omitted.

RULE 5: Use a comma to set off material added to the beginning or end of a sentence.
EXAMPLES:
Because a key witness had died, the case was dismissed.

The appellate courts usually accept the facts as determined by the trial judge, although there are some exceptions.

Frightened, the victim returned to her apartment, screaming for help as she ran.

The comma is not necessary after a short prepositional phrase.

EXAMPLES:
In October the Supreme Court reversed itself.

Inside the apartment the officers found the purple shirt.

Prepositions are words like *with, to, for, under, since,* and *around*. A phrase with only one preposition usually does not require a comma. A phrase with more than one preposition requires a comma.

EXAMPLES:

In October of the preceding year, the Supreme Court reversed itself.

Inside the apartment on 49th Street, the officers found the purple shirt.

The comma is often omitted before material added to the end of a sentence, except when the reader would normally pause before the added material.

EXAMPLES:

The case was dismissed because a key witness had died.

The Supreme Court had reversed itself in October of the preceding year.

The officers found the purple shirt inside the apartment on 49th Street.
BUT
We returned to New York, where the deposition had been taken.

The complainant appealed, perhaps because she was dissatisfied with the amount of the judgment.

When in doubt, read the sentence aloud without pausing before the added material. If the sentence seems rushed without a pause, put the comma in.

RULE 6: Use a colon (:) to mean "to be specific" or "namely and to wit"; use a semicolon (;) to mean "and," "and so," "similarly," or "but."
EXAMPLES:
We find no evidence of an essential element in a conspiracy charge: an overt act setting the plan in motion.

The Fifth Circuit was persuaded that women could guard men in Alabama prisons; the Supreme Court ruled otherwise.

In choosing between a colon and a semicolon, think of these marks as words with specific meanings. If the meaning you want to express is "namely" or "to be specific," use a colon. If it is anything else, use a semicolon.

The meaning "because" can be expressed by either mark.

EXAMPLES:
Judge Tracy felt obliged to excuse himself: the defendant had been his chief opponent in the election.
OR
Judge Tracy felt obliged to excuse himself; the defendant had been his chief opponent in the election.

Since the colon means "namely," it is often used to introduce a list. Because the semicolon means "and," it is often used to separate items in a list.

EXAMPLE:
The case was remanded for three reasons: the defendant was the only Native American in the lineup from which she was identified; she had not been advised of her Miranda rights; and her confession had not been properly signed.

The semicolon is also used along with conjunctive adverbs (words like *however, moreover, furthermore, consequently*) to join two independent clauses.

EXAMPLES:
The trust fund was established in the daughter's name; consequently, she was free to dispose of the money in any way she chose.

The expert had impeccable credentials; her demeanor in court, however, made the jurors mistrust her.

Notice that a conjunctive adverb after a semicolon is always followed by a comma (see "consequently" in the first example above) and that a conjunctive adverb elsewhere in the sentence is set off with a pair of commas (see "however" in the second example above).

RULE 7: Always put commas and periods *before* end quotation marks, even if only a single word is quoted.
EXAMPLE:
They asked to be called "inmates." "Convicts," they said, reminded them of old Bogart movies.

Lawyers have trouble with this rule when they sense that the comma or period is not part of the quoted material. It helps to know that the rule is not logical. It was established in part by Linotype operators, who found it easier to finger a comma or period before a quotation mark than to finger the reverse sequences, and in part by editors, who considered the more logical sequences (". and ",) visually unappealing. Logic, therefore, has nothing to do with this rule. People who read carefully edited prose are so accustomed to seeing commas and periods before end quotation marks that they are disturbed by the reverse sequence, even when the reverse sequence makes more sense. Consequently, the standard stylebooks have made a rule of what began as an illogical convention: "In American usage, with quotation marks, a final comma or period always goes *inside*" (Turabian, *A Manual for Writers*). See also "A Handbook of Style" in *Webster's New Collegiate Dictionary*.

The one necessary exception to this rule occurs when the writer is specifying emendations to a document.

EXAMPLES:
Add the words "gross", "inept", and "startling" in paragraph one.

Add "otherwise" immediately after "may".

If the commas and periods appeared within the end quotation marks, they might turn up in the emended text as well. (See *U.S. Government Printing Office Style Manual*, section 8:147.)

Colons and semicolons, by the way, always go outside end quotation marks:

EXAMPLES:
The jury rejected VanPelt's argument that the money was "just a gift": the check was signed only three days before VanPelt was awarded a contract.

He shouted "Stop!"; apparently the driver could not hear him.

Question marks go inside end quotation marks if they are part of the quoted material, outside if they are not.

EXAMPLES:
The judge turned to the defense and said, "Is this the same list of stipulated facts you presented yesterday?"

Were his exact words "Let's forget about the lease"?

Notice that only one punctuation mark—i.e., one period or one question mark—is necessary at the end of a sentence, even if the quoted material happens to be a sentence in itself.

RULE 8: When quoted material is more than four lines it should be set off from the rest of the text and indented.
EXAMPLE:
In *Arsinger* v. *Hamlin,* Justice Burger pointed out in a concurring opinion that indigents have a right to counsel only when a jail term is actually given:

> Because no individual can be imprisoned unless he is represented by counsel, the trial judge and the prosecutor will have to engage in a predictive evaluation of each case to determine whether there is a likelihood that, if the defendant is convicted, the trial judge will sentence him to a jail term. 407 U.S. 42

Quotations of this sort are called block quotations. The purpose of block quotations is to aid the reader in determining where the quoted material begins and ends; if long quotes were simply enclosed as part of the text—particularly if they were to include more than one sentence—the reader might have difficulty discerning where the quoted material ends.

Notice that block quotations do *not* require the addition of quotation marks; the block form is itself enough to indicate that the material is quoted.

When possible, avoid long quotations if buried within them is a word or phrase that is essential to the argument. Readers tend to skip long quotations, hoping to surmise their content from the material that precedes and follows them. If you want to call attention to a detail in the law, do not hide it by citing the entire law. Long quotations are especially to be avoided if they are so poorly written that they might confuse or delay the reader.

The best practice is to paraphrase the context and to quote only those words or phrases that bear directly on the point at hand. Often when a writer puts "emphasis added" after a long quotation, the only part that should have been quoted is the part to which emphasis has been added. The rest should have been paraphrased.

RULE 9: When part of a quoted sentence is omitted, use three spaced dots to indicate the omission; when the omission occurs after

the last word in the preceding sentence quoted, it is indicated with four dots, the first of which is a period.
EXAMPLE:
As the Court noted in *Whitman* v. *Whitman*, "The fair value of a corporate stock . . . is nearly always a difficult problem. . . . there is no exclusive test or measure of actual value." 34 Wis. (2d) 341

In the example above, the three dots after "stock" indicate that words were omitted within the sentence quoted. Of the four dots after "problem," the first is a period, indicating that "problem" was the last word in the sentence quoted; the other three dots indicate that the first part of the next sentence was omitted.

RULE 10: Use hyphens to join compound nouns or compound modifiers, to prevent excessive duplication of vowels or consonants, and to avoid ambiguity; do not use a hyphen after *very* or after words ending in *-ly*.
EXAMPLE:
According to the president-elect, America's small-business owners had reported surprisingly large third-quarter profits due to an increase in anti-import sentiment.

When in doubt about a hyphenated compound, consult an unabridged dictionary, like *Webster's Third New International*. If a compound is not included in the dictionary, the best source for guidance is *A Manual for Writers of Term Papers, Theses, and Dissertations*, discussed below, which gives detailed technical guidelines for using and omitting hyphens.

One authority has suggested that the hyphen was lost "when English passed into American." But the loss may well be ours when unnatural words result from failure to use this device. Israel Shenker reported in the *New York Times* about one dictionary's attempt to use the word nonnative rather than non-native. Without the hyphen the spelling suggests a pronunciation that not only lacks euphony, as Shenker tell us, but also obscures the meaning of the word.[6]

Our ten rules do not cover all the situations that occur in legal writing. For more unusual situations—Do you punctuate the name of a ship by underlining or using quotation marks? When are foreign words considered part of the English language?—attorneys need to consult the same dictionaries and stylebooks that other professional writers and editors use.

The handiest source is a desk dictionary such as *Webster's New Collegiate Dictionary* or the *American Heritage*. The *American Heritage* has a brief usage note under the entry for each punctuation mark; Webster's has gathered the rules together in an appendix called "A Handbook of Style."

The most respected stylebook among publishers is *A Manual of Style*, now in its twelfth edition (Chicago: University of Chicago Press, 1969). Most of the rules covered in this Chicago style manual are also covered in the briefer (and less expensive) paperback by Kate L. Turabian, *A Manual for Writers of Term Papers, Theses, and Dissertations*, fourth edition (Chicago: University of Chicago Press, 1973). Although the title suggests that Turabian's book is intended primarily for academic circles, it is widely respected by commercial publishers as well because it gives clear, authoritative advice about the thorniest of punctuation problems.

Lawyers who work for the federal government should be aware of the *Style Manual* published by the Government Printing Office, which gives especially useful guidance in preparing legal manuscripts for the printer. Ironically, the least useful source of guidance on questions of punctuation is the distinguished *Harvard Blue Book*, which concerns itself almost exclusively with forms for proper citation.

To end where we began, what source includes the rules that should have guided those judgments that depended upon the interpretation of a punctuation mark? Was the Alabama court correct in its interpretation of a comma? Were the courts in Kentucky, Maine, and Maryland right in their interpretation of punctuation?

Unfortunately, no stylebook on earth covers the rules that judges relied on in those cases. In the Alabama case, the judges inferred the intention of the framers of the Constitution, who clearly wanted to prevent hasty amendments. The interpretation of the effect of the comma was based upon common sense, not on a citable rule in a stylebook. In the Kentucky case, the court interpreted semicolons as it surmised the deceased intended. This may have been a reasonable interpretation, though we would be hard pressed to find it expressed in so many words by any authority. Similarly, in Maine the court took note of sources other than the stylebooks to color the law as they thought it should be colored. The Maryland judge knew his punctuation, in a life-and-death sentence. Style-books do not—cannot—anticipate all the legal tangles that lawyers get themselves into.

Lawyers who want to avoid these tangles can do so easily enough: they can master our ten rules; they can consult standard sources for situations not covered by these rules; and they can rewrite sentences not covered by the rules so that they can be covered. Someone's life may hang in the balance.

4

Organization: Procrusteans and Butterflies

When legal writing is poorly organized, it usually suffers from one of two flaws. The writer may have forced the material into a standard form, stretching and lopping off whatever did not fit, like Procrustes adjusting the size of his guests to match their beds. Or the writer may have simply jotted down facts and comments in a spontaneous sequence, like a butterfly visiting flower after flower, with no apparent itinerary or destination.

Good legal writing is of course neither rigid in form nor entirely spontaneous. Good legal writers are aware of the forms normally followed in each circumstance, but they also know when to depart from the tradition to accommodate the facts of a given case or the requirements of a given audience. In addition to the guidance they can get from the various form books that abound in their profession, lawyers need to understand a few basic principles of organization:

1. Facts have no significance unless they are preceded by an issue.
2. Narrative material is easier to handle for the writer and more interesting for the reader if it is presented in chronological order.
3. Descriptive material has no natural or inevitable order.
4. Most legal arguments can be arranged in a simple dialectical structure.

5. The organization of documents concerned with past events requires different and more complex strategies than the organization
of documents concerned with future events.

Once attorneys grasp these principles, they can learn to use the
form books proper to their agencies and jurisdictions without being
slaves to them. They can learn to organize major documents like
briefs, opinions, and formal memoranda coherently, and to write
introductions to them that foreshadow the organization of what
is to come. They can also learn to put the principles to work even
in such routine documents as letters and informal memos.

The first principle—that issues should precede facts—may come
as a surprise to some attorneys. They assume that since the facts
of a case occur first historically (before the client even walks into
the office), they should be presented first on paper, and the issues
that arise out of the facts should be presented later. The problem
with this assumption is that it makes for very inefficient reading.
Facts have no interest, no meaning, unless they are presented in
the context of issues. Nothing is more tedious than reading pages
crammed with apparently random information. If the facts include
precise data (figures, dates, times) and even conflicting data (facts
alleged by one witness juxtaposed with incompatible facts alleged
by another), the reader is obliged to memorize everything until
the necessary context is provided—sometimes many pages later,
sometimes not at all. Imagine, for example, a legal document beginning with a list of facts like the ones below. At what point does
the reader know the relative significance of the details?

1. Crescent City Construction Company built a motel for Recreation Enterprises, an Alabama corporation.
2. The motel was located in Gulf Shores.
3. Construction was completed on June 15, 1976.
4. Final payment for construction was made on July 15, 1976.
5. The total cost of construction was $347,590.76.
6. According to Joel Whitehead, manager of the motel, Crescent
City had not removed some of its equipment, including a
portable generator, a table saw, and assorted handtools, until
August 23, 1976.
7. According to Gerald Richard, president of Crescent City, the
generator and the handtools were the property of a subcontractor,
Seashore Woodworks, a corporation that declared bankruptcy on
July 15, 1976.

8. Richard contends that Crescent City removed the equipment at the request of Whitehead.
9. Whitehead contends that the equipment actually belonged to Crescent City as a result of a verbal agreement made between that company and Seashore Woodworks shortly before the bankruptcy.
10. On August 1, 1976, Ms. Cornelia Jones injured her foot on a rake left buried in the sand by construction workers.
11. Ms. Jones was a registered guest at nearby Surfside Manor.
12. The rake was between the shoreline and the new motel built by Crescent City for Recreation Enterprises.
13. Ms. Jones brought suit in Baldwin County against Crescent City.
14. Crescent City's home office is in New Orleans.

What is a reader to make of this list? Assuming that the case is on appeal and that these facts appear at the beginning of a brief or of the opinion itself, which of these facts are important and which are background information? Is the cost of the construction significant? Is the ownership of the tools essential information? Is the fact that Ms. Jones was registered at a different motel relevant to the appeal? The reader has no way of knowing until the writer indicates the context by announcing the issue; depending upon the issue, the relative importance of the facts will shift. If the issue in this case is whether Crescent City is subject to the long-arm statute, then facts 2, 5, 13, and 14, which indicate the size of the project and the locations relevant to the law, are essential, and the rest are relatively minor. But if the issue is whether the accident was a foreseeable consequence of Crescent City's action, then the location of the rake (facts 10 and 12) and the dispute about the ownership of the tools (facts 6–9), which would be unimportant in the context of other issues, suddenly become essential. And if the issue on appeal is whether Crescent City could be held responsible for the rake afer construction had been completed and paid for, the dates in facts 3, 4, and 10 assume an importance they would not have under the other issues.

A well-organized document should therefore present the issues first so the reader has some sense of the relative importance of each fact as it is mentioned.

The second principle—that narrative material should be presented in chronological order—is not as obvious as it might seem. After all, our memory of things past is not a smooth ribbon of events, but as Proust and Faulkner portray it, an associative odyssey in which each remembered event triggers a connection with some other, either earlier or later in time. The following passage, for example, was written in one of our seminars by an attorney who had been given an oral presentation of facts and procedural history in a hypothetical case. The attorney apparently wrote down the events in the sequence in which he remembered them rather than in the sequence in which they had occurred:

> The Court decided that it had authority to issue the writ. The parents of Julie Necaise asked the Court to issue a writ of habeas corpus ordering the Church of the Moon to bring forth their daughter so that they could determine whether she was being restrained by psychological coercion. A hearing was held to determine whether the writ shall be issued. The Court refused to issue the writ because the Necaises had not established that the Church of the Moon was restraining their daughter by psychological means. Evidence was heard as to whether the Court had jurisdiction in the matter. The Court decided that it did have jurisdiction.

Unless they are given time to study this passage closely, most readers might have trouble following it. It is not clear how many hearings were held, nor in what sequence the Court made its findings. The first event to take place is mentioned in sentence 2—the parents asked for a writ. The second is in sentence 3—the Court held a hearing. The third event, the presentation of evidence regarding the Court's jurisdiction, is mentioned in sentence 5. The fourth event, the Court's determination that it did in fact have jurisdiction, is mentioned twice, in sentences 1 and 6. And the climax of the story, the Court's refusal to issue the writ, is buried in sentence 4.

Arranged chronologically, the habeas corpus case makes better sense:

> The parents of Julie Necaise asked the Court to issue a writ of habeas corpus ordering the Church of the Moon to bring forth their daughter so that they could determine whether she was being restrained by psychological coercion. A hearing was held to determine whether the writ should be issued. Evidence was heard as to whether the Court had jurisdiction in the matter. The Court decided that it did have

jurisdiction. It refused to issue the writ because the Necaises had not established that the Church of the Moon was restraining their daughter by psychological means.

The revision is not immortal prose, but it is much easier to read than the original. In addition to rearranging the sentences in chronological order, the only alterations were to eliminate the first sentence entirely, to change "shall be issued" to "should be issued," and to change "The Court" to "it." Why each change was required is significant. Unnecessary repetition is a common sign of poor organization. The writer would not have been tempted to repeat the information in sentence 1 if the passage had been properly organized. Nor would the writer have stumbled on a tough choice between "should" and "shall" in sentence 3 if the passage had been organized chronologically. Chronological order usually enables the writer to avoid tough grammatical questions about sequences of tenses and propriety of modals, questions that even professional editors and grammarians have trouble answering with confidence.

The third principle—that descriptive material has no natural or inevitable order—runs contrary to common textbook advice that descriptive passages should follow a logical sequence. Actually, the best writers often arrange details in descriptive passages in random or associative patterns—precisely those patterns that will not work well for narrative material. Although a logical sequence such as left to right or top to bottom is often useful in a descriptive passage, the sequence is not as important as the writer's choice of details to convey the impression or information that the writer wants to convey. In legal writing, the purpose of description is always to enable the reader to make a judgment. When description in the law is faulty, the cause of the problem is usually the omission of essential details. Here, for example, is a passage from a case in which the issue was whether the arresting officer could have been close enough to a patch of marijuana to identify it without first obtaining a warrant to search property the defendant had rented from one Mr. Smith, who was also the informant in the case.

Mr. Smith's house was located immediately to the south of the defendant's house and the two were separated by a fence. Immediately to the west there was a private lane which exited Fourth

Avenue in Meridian, and proceeded north to a bar located on the property. Immediately to the north and east of defendant's house was an old hen house with an enclosed chicken yard. Just beyond the chicken house was the eastern boundary line of the property, which extended to the north. Beyond the boundaries on the north and east sides there were nothing but open fields. The farm property to the east of the chicken yard was a large open pasture, owned also by Mr. Smith.

The description is pleasant enough—an inviting, bucolic scene. Most of it, in fact, the reader could sketch in a rudimentary map: the east-west fence separating the landlord's property from the tenant's; the landlord's house below the fence, the tenant's house and chicken coop above; another fence running along the eastern border of the land, extending far to the north into open fields. A pretty picture. The only thing missing from the description is an indication of the shortest distance from which the officer could have viewed the crop without obstruction and without trespassing on land rented to the defendant. Without this information, the reader cannot judge whether the officer could have viewed the greenery closely enough to identify it without first having obtained a search warrant.

Like narration, description can sometimes serve purposes that are rhetorically justified, even though the matter described has little or nothing to do with the case at bar. A judge on the Supreme Court of Mississippi once showed us his description of a power plant in which a construction worker had fallen to his death. The judge had spent days on the passage, even going to the trouble of bringing a model of the plant into his office so he could study it as he wrote. The description was still impossible to follow. We showed him how the description could have been made clearer and much briefer, but we also pointed out that the entire section could have been eliminated entirely, since the issue on appeal was whether the power company or the construction company was in control of the plant when the accident occurred. The layout of the plant had nothing to do with the case. "Well," the judge conceded, "I suppose you're right. But I'd do it the same way again if I had the chance. Some of my brethren on the bench were inclined to vote the other way on this decision, but those five pages sufficiently confused them until they started seeing things right."

We are often asked about how much detail to include in narrative and descriptive passages. When do details enrich and enliven writing, and when do they load it down and bore the reader? The line between too much and not enough is not always easy to draw, but the principle to keep in mind is whether the details are important to the purpose of what is being written. If, for example, a defense attorney is writing a brief in a case in which self-defense is the issue, there would be reason for writing a paragraph like this:

The Murray farm was situated in an isolated rural area outside town. Ms. Murray was a widow, eighty years old, who lived alone. On the night of October 16, Ms. Murray was in her house, asleep in her room on the third floor. There was no moon. The night was silent. Sometime after midnight, Ms. Murray heard squeaky sounds from the back staircase that led to the hallway outside her door. The sounds got louder. She reached to her nightstand and took out a pistol her husband had given her many years earlier. Suddenly the door to her bedroom sprang open. She saw a large figure that seemed menacing to her. Petrified, she pulled the trigger and shot at the figure that stepped in her direction.

Here the details serve the purpose of creating a mood that needed to be established for Ms. Murray to have claimed self-defense when she was charged with murdering her nephew, who was driving home from college and needed a place to stay for the evening. The details do more to establish a vicarious feeling about Ms. Murray's state of mind at the time she shot her nephew than simply stating the conclusion that she was shocked and frightened under the circumstances. The proper use of details can bring the reader along with the writer and lead to the conclusion the writer desires.

Details can also be useful to the prosecution. A county attorney in Michigan, for example, once showed us a brief he had submitted in a rape and murder case that had been appealed. The defendant claimed that certain photographs had been used improperly to help witnesses identify him in the lineup. The brief for the prosecution included a detailed account of the crime, which was a particularly gory one. Theoretically one could argue that these details had nothing to do with the issue on appeal and should have been omitted. The appellate judge certainly should have ignored them, since the right to due process applies to all defendants, regardless of the nature of the charge. The details did, however, serve the purpose of reminding the judge that this particular defendant was extraordinarily dangerous, not at all deserving the benefit of any doubts his attorney might raise about the propriety of the investigation. The conviction was sustained; the details, no doubt, served their purpose.

Sometimes, however, lawyers load down their prose with details that serve no purpose. For example, if a prosecutor's brief concerns the propriety of a police officer's search of a trunk of a car and the discovery of contraband, there would be no need to lead into the arrest in this fashion:

> Officers Peter A. O'Toole and John A. Jones were driving their police cruiser in an easterly direction on Route 142A, heading out of downtown Zenith in the direction of the community of Outer Zenith. They turned left at the corner of Elm and Maple and were proceeding in the direction of West Cupcake when they noticed a car speeding. . . .

None of the details mentioned here are relevant to the issue, which is whether the officers who stopped a speeding driver had probable cause to search his trunk. In fact, the details serve only to distract the reader.

The fourth principle—that legal arguments can be arranged in a simple dialectical structure—gets to the heart of legal writing, the point and counterpoint, thrust and parry, that make or break each case. Once the facts of the case have been laid out in narrative and descriptive passages, the business of analysis begins. No matter how complex or controversial a case may be, the structure of analysis is always the same, a simple alternation between a thesis and an antithesis, applied to every issue that counsel for either side chooses to raise. One side says X is the controlling law applicable to the facts; the other side says X does not quite fit the facts. In organizing briefs, then, the attorney's job is always the same: first decide on the issues that either side intends to raise and arrange them in logical order; then repeat the dialectical pattern (thesis/antithesis) for each issue, explaining first the application of law urged by opposing counsel, and then why the law (or the distinctions) urged by opposing counsel are wrong. For judges, the pattern usually involves explaining the position of losing party first, and then explaining and affirming the position of prevailing party. Sometimes, of course, judges are inclined to add a third element to the dialectic, saying in effect that one side argues X, the other argues Y, but the truth of the matter is Z. The Z, of course, may be a synthesis of some sort, or even a new position entirely; but in either case, its logical position in the document is after the judge has explained X and Y.

A common mistake among attorneys and judges is to demean the opposing or losing point of view by expressing it weakly or by dismissing it as "frivolous" or absolutely without merit or rationale when in fact it may well have presented, however ineptly, some points worthy of consideration. Attorneys can discover the strengths and weaknesses of their own cases if they express the opposite position so clearly and forcefully that the opposition itself would be pleased. When they feel they can refute the logic of an argument expressed as cogently as possible, they have a case; when they feel the need to demean an argument rather than to dismantle it neatly, they are taking risks that would be better avoided.

When a case involves several issues, treating them in the proper sequence requires careful strategy. Sometimes issues are entirely independent of one another and can be discussed in a random sequence. Sometimes the issues are a logical chain, in which the discussion of each issue depends upon the resolution of another. Sometimes one issue holds the key to all the others; normally that issue should be settled first.

We found a case in Tennessee in which the dispositive issue was whether the defendant had standing in court. After meticulous rulings on thirteen other issues, the judge ruled on the last page that because the plaintiff had filed certain papers after the deadline he had lost his standing. That, we suggested, should have been the first issue to be settled, since it made discussion of the others unnecessary. "No," the judge countered, "I settled the other issues first so that if I am overruled, the Supreme Court will have my judgment on everything else, and the litigants will be spared the expense of further court action." No one can argue with the judge's good intentions. It would have been better, however, if he had announced his plan on page 1, settled the dispositive issue first, and then dealt with the others beginning with a transition like "Even if the plaintiff had standing, the other issues ..."

The fifth principle of organization—that documents concerned with the past require strategies different from those required by documents concerned with the future—is distantly related to a distinction made by Aristotle, who divided legal writing into three categories according to the time frame of their subject matter: past (which he called judical discourse); present (which he called epideictic discourse); and future (which he called deliberative or legislative discourse). The second category, which is sometimes called ceremonial discourse, is related more to the political side of the law than to the technical side. But the distinction between the other two categories—between writing about the past and writing about the future—has practical implications for the organization of everyday legal writing.

Documents that deal with events in the future—prospective documents such as statutes, wills, and contracts—are essentially reference documents. The main objective in organizing documents of this sort is to enable the reader to locate any particular provision when there is a need to apply it to a set of facts. The provisions within documents of this sort can often be presented as lists of independent items, like entries in an encyclopedia or a dictionary, or grouped together in logical categories with appropriate headings and arranged in almost any sequence, as long as there are sufficient signposts to guide future readers in their search for particular details.

Occasionally, of course, logic and common sense will dictate that some provisions ought to precede others: definitions, for example, should precede the use of the words defined; and in "if/then" sequences (e.g., if the price of raw materials should rise, then the buyer shall have the option of absorbing the increased cost or rescinding the contract), the "if" portion should precede the "then" portion. Except in circumstances like these, however, there may be no inherent sequence the writer must respect. The writer's primary purpose in choosing a pattern of organization is to make it easy for future readers to find what they are looking for. Handbooks and guidelines for documents of this kind are so abundant that it would be impractical to list them all here. As a general guide, attorneys can find models in *Legal Forms* and *Legal Forms 2d*, both published by the Lawyers' Cooperative. Virtually every jurisdiction in the United States, however, has more particular guidelines, including weighty annotated tomes, some dedicated to a single form (wills, for example, or contracts). These works vary in quality, but their common value is that they list the elements required to make a particular kind of document legally sound, and they show how these elements are traditionally arranged.

Retrospective writing—writing that deals with facts from the past—includes memoranda, motions, complaints, indictments, briefs, judgments, and decisions. The purpose of this kind of writing is almost always either to explain or to persuade. As opposed to lists of more or less independent provisions, they should be meticulously designed engines of logic, applying one or several theories of law to the facts at hand. Like the inner workings of a clock, each part has an indispensable function, and the others cannot work well without it. Attorneys cannot afford to arrange the parts haphazardly, hoping their readers will be cagey enough to begin at the end and skip back to the middle, or patient enough to read the whole thing through once just to locate the important parts and then again with sympathetic attention to the writer's best arguments. There are form books for this kind of writing, too, the most general of which is *American Jurisprudence Pleading and Practice Forms*, also published by the Lawyers Cooperative. And each jurisdiction has its own more particular guidelines, sometimes published under the general title "Rules of Court," and sometimes under more particular titles, like "Rules for Appellate Procedure" or "Federal Complaint Forms." Usually these books are based on principles of logic, rhetoric, and common sense.

In anything attorneys write, one or several of these five principles will be applicable. All of them are at work in every full appellate decision. As retrospective documents, appellate decisions require tight logical relationships among their various subsections. They include disputes about one or several issues that have to be announced early and arranged in a logical sequence. Facts are rarely arguable on appeal, but the facts found or stipulated in trial must be set out in the decision in either a narrative or a descriptive passage (sometimes both). And appellate decisions always include the sort of arguments and counterarguments that can be arranged in a dialectical structure.

Everything attorneys write—from the simplest office memo to the most complex legislation—ought to be written as if it were certain to be examined in an appellate court. The appeals court ultimately determines what a document means (regardless of the author's intentions), and its decision determines whether the document is enforceable. For these reasons, we usually begin our discussion of organization with a model outline for an appellate decision. Once attorneys have mastered this form, it is relatively easy for them to apply the principle behind it to the shorter forms that make up the bulk of their written work.

The outline we suggest for decisions is this:

I. Beginning
II. Narration of facts
III. Application of law
IV. Summary, judgment, order, recommendation, etc.

Students of the law will recognize that this outline resembles what is recommended by many of the standard "Rules for Appellate Procedure." Although these rules are written primarily as instructions for attorneys preparing appellate briefs, the fact that they work for opinions as well indicates that these two forms—briefs and opinions—are closely related, their essential difference being that judges have the authority to conclude with decisions while attorneys can conclude only with pleadings.

In all legal writing, beginnings are extremely important. Attorneys should regard each first page as prime real estate. What they put there ought to be worth the space it occupies. Nothing wastes this space more outrageously than the standard boilerplate some judges consider essential, the ritualistic incantation borrowed either from outmoded form books or from the traditional practice in jurisdictions that have never bothered to examine their traditions with a critical eye. Here is an example we found in Idaho, written by a judge who dispatched every case in exactly the same way, inserting the names and dates at hand between long stretches of high jargon:

THIS MATTER having come before this Court on the basis of briefs submitted to the Court in chambers and Counsel having waived oral argument on said matter, Plaintiff appearing by counsel and having submitted a brief in Support of Plaintiff's Motion and Defendant appearing by Counsel and having submitted a brief Opposing the Motion to Dismiss and a Reply Brief, the Court having considered the motions, affidavits and briefs, finds as follows:

What followed, predictably, was a section called "Findings of Facts," in which a good story was chopped up and served as a series of unrelated sentences; another section, called "Conclusions of Law," in which the reader found the results of the judge's deliberations without any indication of the logic supporting them; and a final section called "Judgment," which was probably the only section the attorneys and their clients bothered to read, either with delight or dismay (depending upon their point of view), but certainly not with understanding.

The purpose of a beginning is to arouse the interest and sympathy of the audience and to provide the context necessary for understanding the rest of the document. For this reason, the beginning of every brief and opinion should include these three elements:

1. the nature of the case, including a general statement indicating who did what to whom.
2. the nature and number of issues.
3. an explicit or implicit indication of the organization of the rest of the document.

Some judges like to mention the result of their deliberations in the opening paragraphs; others prefer to postpone the conclusion until the last paragraph, on the theory that readers will follow the logic of the opinion without bias if they do not know in advance where it will lead. Both strategies have merit; but because attorneys generally read the last page of opinions first (or if the opinion is published, they read the editor's summary first), it makes little practical difference where the conclusion is placed.

One of the most common mistakes attorneys make is to fail to indicate who did what to whom at the outset. There are important psychological reasons for grounding every legal document in the human conflict that precedes it. First, all of us find it much easier to follow the abstract reasoning required in legal controversies if we can imagine the concrete reality—the brutal murder, the devious dealings, the leaky pipes and spoiled merchandise—to which the abstractions are being applied. Second, all readers are naturally interested in stories, especially stories that involve conflicts between human beings or conflicts between human beings and their environment. And finally, the reader's sympathy is more likely to be aroused if the case is presented as a concrete injustice being perpetrated on an innocent victim than if it is presented as a technical violation of an abstract code. At the heart of every legal action is a good story. Although lawyers can't tell these stories in exactly the same way novelists or journalists would tell them, it is foolish to ignore their dramatic interest or to postpone telling them until the reader is already lulled into deep sleep by a mindless liturgy invoking the names of all the attorneys and their firms and the rules of procedure that were the cause of this gathering together in the name of the law, world without end, amen.

By "beginning" we mean the first page (or if the first page is taken up by mandatory style, the equivalent of a first page). Since beginnings have to do several things in addition to telling who did what to whom, there won't be enough space to tell the entire story at the beginning. The details have to be saved for Part II, "Narration of Facts." Somewhere on the first page, however, should be a simple description of the human conflict in terms that are neither too general ("This is a murder case") nor too specific ("On October 31, 1981, A.D., defendant, who resides at 1313 Heathcliff Avenue, and who in this case is represented by Strunk and White, attorneys at law, was seen walking in a northerly direction down the east side of . . .").

As an example of a good beginning, consider the paragraph below. It was written by the honorable Jesse R. Walters, now chief justice of the Idaho Court of Appeals. Although it was written for a decision, it would serve just as well as a first paragraph in a brief.

The defendant stands charged with a series of burglary, kidnapping, rape and battery incidents which allegedly occurred in 1976 and 1978. In the majority of the cases, the assailant was masked, gloved and wore a hooded covering over his head, preventing the victims from visually observing the facial features of the assailant. Only the eyes of the assailant were uncovered. Following the arrest of the defendant on November 11, 1978, several lineup confrontations were arranged by the police for the victims, using a number of subjects including the defendant, for the purpose of identifying the assailant.

The defendant has moved for suppression of the evidence of lineup identification by the victims mainly upon three grounds, i.e. (1) that one or more of the lineups were conducted without the defendant's counsel being present; (2) that the people in the lineup wore clothing which had been illegally seized from the defendant's automobile; and (3) that the lineups were suggestive.

We concede that a fastidious editor would find faults in this passage; nevertheless, as a beginning it is first-rate. The first paragraph states a conflict in a way that engages the reader's interest and provides the factual context necessary for the rest of the document to make sense. It is neither so general that it could apply to any rape case that ever occurred nor so specific that it bogs down in excessive detail. In style it is clean and direct. It is neither overwritten nor so dry as to be devoid of interest.

The second paragraph announces the issues, but instead of saying "The issues on appeal are . . ." the judge uses the subtler technique of mentioning the three grounds upon which the defendant moves for the suppression of evidence in the order in which the judge intends to discuss them, so the reader will know what sort of facts to look for in the narrative section and what legal arguments to anticipate in the discussion. In this particular decision, the beginning was followed by a brief narration describing the lineup and the police procedures in appropriate detail, and then by a discussion of the issues foreshadowed in the second paragraph under three headings: "Absence of Counsel," "Clothing," and "Lineup-Suggestibility." Nothing could have been clearer.

Foreshadowing the issues is possible and desirable even when there are multiple issues to be decided. Almost always, multiple issues can be divided into a few categories and foreshadowed as groups of related issues:

> The appellant raises fifty issues on appeal. Twenty deal with the pretrial investigation. Fifteen deal with jury selection. The remaining fifteen deal with instructions the judge gave or refused to give to the jury.

A passage like this early in a brief or opinion gives the reader a sense of orderliness in what would otherwise seem like a bewildering thicket of random arguments.

After a beginning that engages the reader's interest and provides the context for the rest of the document, the next section is the detailed narration of facts and other background information that must precede the application of law. Once the issues have been enunciated, the facts ought to be interesting, especially if they are told in a continuous narrative, like any good story. Lawyers can make them uninteresting, however, if they chop the action into small bits, as we did in the Crescent City Construction case above, add a few irrelevant details, and after jumbling the events to remove any hint of chronology, hang them out in an enumerated list. In this way a Saturday night brawl can be made as lively as Monday morning's laundry.

The very form—enumerated facts—guarantees boredom. Attorneys and judges who use this form insist that it is required by some rule of law. Or if they concede that enumeration is not required, they defend it as a handy device, allowing subsequent references to be expressed precisely.

We are not persuaded by these arguments. In every jurisdiction in which we have heard enumeration described as an absolute requirement by some attorney or trial judge, we have found other attorneys and trial judges happily presenting their facts in narrative form without enumeration and without reprimands or reversals from on high. The argument about convenience in subsequent references is an illusion. It is never useful to refer to a finding solely by its number; the fact itself will have to be described, as in "The fact that construction was completed in June (see Findings, number 3) . . ." As long as the fact has to be summarized, one might just as well have the parenthetical reference read "See Findings, p. 2," which is precise enough as a reference for even the most rigorous scholarly journals.

The advantages to be gained by not enumerating facts are readability and interest, enabling readers to stay awake for the legal discussion without pinching themselves. In the law, interest is not just an end in itself: it is a means of persuasion. Good writing, like good speech, captures the audience. Here, for example, is how a disorderly conduct charge that went all the way to the U.S. Supreme Court was handled by the late Associate Justice William O. Douglas.

Petitioner after jury trial was found guilty of disorderly conduct in violation of a city ordinance of Chicago and fined. The case grew out of an address he delivered in an auditorium in Chicago under the auspices of the Christian Veterans of America. The meeting commanded considerable public attention. The auditorium was filled to capacity with over eight hundred persons present. Others were turned away. Outside of the auditorium a crowd of about one thousand persons gathered to protest against the meeting. A cordon of policemen was assigned to the meeting to maintain order; but they were not able to prevent several disturbances. The crowd outside was angry and turbulent.[1]

To be sure, not every case has the immediate allure of physical conflict. But every case that goes to court—criminal or civil—has the essential element of drama in it: a conflict of human minds and wills. Whether the story involves a tavern brawl, a real estate scam, an ambiguous will, a questionable corporate merger, or a wrinkle in the tax code, there is always dramatic conflict at the core of the case, and the fact that the litigants bother to take the dispute to court is proof that the stakes are high enough to be interesting. Whenever a legal conflict cannot be made interesting as a narrative, counsel for one side has made a mistake. Either the matter is too trivial or the law too clearly settled to justify the trouble and expense of litigation.

Part III of our model outline calls for "Application of Law." In Part III lawyers explain—often discovering as they write—how current law applies or fails to apply to the facts. To write Part III, attorneys should begin by imagining that their readers have dropped into the office and said, "Listen, I'm in a big hurry and I won't have time to read what you are about to write. Why don't you just tell me in a nutshell what this case is about and how it should be resolved." The answer should be something like this: "To make a long story short, defendant has apparently done thus and so (the facts). Opposing counsel claims that this sort of behavior is subject to such and such law (theory X), but we reject this argument for these reasons (theory Y)."

That simple pattern—essential facts, application of the law as one party sees it, and application of the law as another party sees it—is the heart of every brief and opinion. It may of course be necessary to repeat this pattern several times if the defendant has done a number of suspicious things or if one of the attorneys wants to raise a number of legal questions. When the pattern has to be repeated this way, the case obviously involves multiple issues, one for each time the pattern is repeated.

Just as attorneys are often uncertain about how many details they ought to include in descriptive and narrative sections of their writing, they often have problems deciding how full they should make their discussion sections. Attorneys sometimes feel compelled to respond to every argument opposing counsel could possibly raise, no matter how frivolous. Sometimes, of course, they err in the opposite direction, by not responding to opposing arguments that turn out to be persuasive to the judge. Judges, too, often have difficulty deciding between too much and not enough. We know a judge in Georgia, for example, who insists upon including in his decisions reams of facts that have no bearing on the case because on one occasion, he tells us, he was reversed on a decision that said simply, "Defendant is guilty of two counts of armed robbery as charged and hereby sentenced to ten years of hard labor." Having once failed in his legal responsibility to provide the essential shape of the case, he resolved to fail from then on by punishing the appellate courts with useless paperwork.

Two principles should guide attorneys in this matter. The first has to do with persuasion, the second with making a document stand on its own.

In an ideal world, one as precise and logical as a mathematical theorem, logic would tell attorneys and judges the difference between solid and faulty lines of reasoning. In an ideal world, frivolous arguments would seem frivolous to any reasonable person who examined them. But law does not operate in an ideal world. Reasonable and intelligent people often disagree about the relative merit of legal theories. When attorneys want to be persuasive, then, they need to be acutely aware of the sort of arguments their readers —trial judges, superior courts, the press—are likely to consider valid. It is small consolation for an attorney who loses a case or a judge who is reversed to hear, "Oh well, that happened because the judge was influenced by a line of argument that really should not have been allowed in court." Part of effective legal writing is knowing and anticipating the sort of arguments that are likely to be taken seriously by the various and varied individuals who make up the legal system. Of course, overloading the document—piling fact upon fact, argument upon argument, in hopes that if one line of reasoning does not impress the court, another one will—is no way to solve the problem. The arguments most likely to persuade the court may get lost in the thicket.

The second principle for determining how full a discussion section should be is that ordinarily, documents should be self-contained. A reader unfamiliar with the case ought to be able to read the document from top to bottom and understand the significance of every detail along the way. Theoretically, a motion, a brief, or even an opinion can serve its immediate purpose if the persons to whom it is addressed—the judge, the attorneys, the litigants— can make sense of it. But these readers have an advantage in reading, since they already know what the case is about and what the document is likely to contain. The immediate audience, therefore, is a relatively easy audience to satisfy.

In practice, however, legal documents have a way of turning up in the hands of readers who are not intimately familiar with the case: the appellate court, for example, or the press, or law students, or subsequent generations of attorneys who for some reason have to unravel the threads of legal reasoning long after the writers have forgotten the details or become unavailable to discuss them. For this reason, we urge attorneys to put enough information in every document to enable perfect strangers to make sense of it even though they were not involved in the actual proceedings.

Although our outline calls for a beginning, a narrative, and a discussion, in that order, the discussion section should ordinarily be written first. The beginning cannot be written first, since it has to foreshadow what is to come and foreshadowing a discussion that hasn't yet been written is impossible. Nor can you write a narration of essential facts before discovering, by writing the discussion section, which of the many facts you have at hand have any bearing on the legal questions being raised.

Part IV of our outline is the conclusion, which takes different forms in different kinds of documents. In opinions, the conclusion may consist of "Conclusions of Law" and "Order," or some other statement indicating what the judge has decided and what the litigants are required to do as a result. This section is usually too brief to present serious organizational problems, although judges should be careful to see that each issue raised earlier in the opinion is matched with a corresponding conclusion of law. An issue is, after all, by definition the sort of question that judges are asked to decide. It would make no sense to raise issues in an opinion and then leave them unsettled.

In briefs the conclusion is essentially a recommendation. Often the recommendation can be stated in a single sentence: "For the reasons explained above, plaintiff moves that the verdict reached by the jury be set aside." If the brief is more than a few pages, however, it makes sense to review the logical chain that leads to the conclusion, so that if a busy reader had time to read only the first section and the last, these two alone would provide the gist of the argument within.

In some offices—particularly in governmental agencies and large private firms—most attorneys have few occasions to draft full briefs or opinions. For them, the most difficult writing task is the formal memorandum, usually addressed to lead attorneys, senior partners, or commissioners, and usually recommending tactics to be followed in a particular case. These memoranda can be as short as a single page or as long as several hundred, depending upon the nature of the case. Whenever a memorandum is longer than two pages, organization becomes a major problem for the writer.

Outlining formal memoranda is similar in principle to outlining briefs and opinions, but different in detail. The outline we suggest is this:

   I. Beginning
  II. Background
 III. Discussion
 IV. Summary and conclusion

The beginning of a formal memorandum is every bit as important as the beginning of an opinion or brief. It should say who did want to whom, it should indicate the nature and number of issues to be discussed, and it should somehow foreshadow the structure of what is to follow. It should not be wasted on technical distinctions, unnecessary ritual, or elaborate philosophical speculation.

A common mistake in writing beginnings for memoranda is to start in medias res, right in the thick of a legal battle from the distant past, without any indication of why this precedent would be of any value to the case at hand. Here, for example, is an opening paragraph written by an attorney in a federal agency. It starts out as if the writer had been interrupted in his research and offered a penny for his thoughts.

The holding of *Federal Maritime Commission* v. *DeSmedt*, 366 F.2d 464 (2d. Cir.), *cert. denied*, 385 U.S. 974 (1966), is clear and unequivocal. The court found that §27 of the Shipping Act authorized the Federal Maritime Commission to: subpoena documents wherever located, and that the words "from any place in the United States" were designed to expand the Commission's subpoena power beyond territorial limits once imposed by the Judicial Code and presently by Fed. R. Civ. P. 45(e), rather than to restrict the Commission's subpoena power to documents located in the United States. 366 F.2d at 368.

It is impossible to guess what relevance this discussion will eventually have. It is also impossible to guess what is likely to occur next. It is not impossible to guess, however, that the person to whom this memorandum was addressed would have preferred to have gotten a clear and coherent view of the case from the outset, rather than a random bit of information, like a piece from a jigsaw puzzle, that would make sense only when all the other pieces had been put in their right places.

Sometimes a particular memorandum is part of a steady flow of correspondence in which it would be superfluous to remind the reader who did what to whom. The mere mention of the names of the litigants is sufficient reminder. Under these circumstances, a reminder of the nature of the case is unnecessary, and the beginning takes on a new purpose, which is to enable the reader to answer these three questions before finishing page 1: "What case are we dealing with?"; "What does the writer want me to do as a result of reading this document?"; and "Why?" Here is an example of a beginning that would work very nicely in a memorandum from an investigating attorney to a lead attorney in a law firm or government agency:

> To enable us to prove negligence in construction at Smitherman Academy, I recommend that we hire Crossland Laboratories to test the strength of the concrete block used in the portion of the auditorium that collapsed.

After a beginning, the reader is in a position to evaluate the arguments that support the recommendation without first wandering through a maze of apparently pointless information about the physics of construction work, the history of Crossland Laboratories, or other information that might be relevant to the decision. Some writers are even less subtle about indicating what they want the reader to do: they type the word RECOMMENDATION in caps at the top of the page, where it fairly shouts for the attention of even the busiest reader:

> RECOMMENDATION: After investigating the facts likely to be available to the prosecution in the McKinley case, I recommend that we move to bar admission of the defendant's purple shirt as evidence, since it is the only hard evidence linking McKinley to the robbery, and it was confiscated without a warrant.

This plain, simple, workaday opening would be much more useful to a senior attorney working on the case than the sort of leisurely opening that former law review editors are tempted to write, beginning with a history of the rules of evidence and considering every conceivable alternative before revealing the problem and the course of action recommended. Similarly, if the lead attorney concurs with the memorandum, the judge would be grateful to see a motion beginning with the request rather than with a detailed review of the case, the rules, and the calling cards of the attorneys. A motion might reasonably begin with a straightforward statement of what is being moved:

> Defendant, Michael McKinley, respectfully petitions the Court to bar any reference to the defendant's purple shirt during these proceedings, since the shirt was confiscated from the defendant's apartment in a search without a warrant.

After such a beginning, a brief narration of the facts surrounding the search and a brief discussion of the law governing searches will make perfect sense to the reader. There is no need to point out that Michael McKinley does not make this motion himself, and that he has his attorneys do his legal work for him. The judge knows that. And unless the motion depends on some particularly obscure provision of the law, there is no point in citing the rules under which it is made. If the motion is inconsistent with the rules, the judge or the opposing counsel will certainly inform the movant; if it is consistent with the rules and if the rules are fairly well known, no judge will deny the petition because the rule was not cited in the first paragraph. In fact, unless citation of the rule is a specific requirement of a particular jurisdiction, it may very well be omitted from the petition entirely.

Briefs and opinions are often written with a kind of healthy paranoia; attorneys are keenly aware of the possibility that disgruntled litigants, superior courts, and the press may pounce like ravenous tigers on any lapse in logic or phraseology. Formal memoranda ought to be written in much the same way, even though their audience—senior partners in the firm, supervising attorneys or commissioners in an agency—may be presumed to be sympathetic to the writer's point of view. If these readers are doing their jobs well, they will scrutinize each tactic proposed in a memorandum for flaws that opposing counsel could turn to their own advantage. Even though the actual audience of a memorandum is friendly, it ought to be written as if it were directed to the most skeptical reader the writer could imagine. It ought to anticipate and counter every reasonable objection, every reasonable alternative. As in most things for which "reasonable" is the measure of appropriateness, there are two ways to err: by overdoing it—that is, by wasting time dealing with objections that no reasonable person would raise; and by underdoing it—that is, by failing to anticipate objections that a person in authority would be obliged to consider.

As important as they are, briefs, opinions, motions, and memoranda are only a small part of the writing associated with lawyers. Equally important, and in some cases equally voluminous, are the letters attorneys write. The substance of these letters is infinite in variety. The most common motives for writing legal letters, however, are to request information or to respond to such a request; to allege grievances or to respond to alleged grievances; to negotiate the settlement of a dispute or the terms of an agreement; to establish procedures to be followed in court or facts to be stipulated at trial; to transmit other documents along with instructions about how they are to be used. A full treatment of the art of legal letter writing would require a volume in itself, but the arrangement of these letters is generally easier than the organization of longer forms, since there is less material to organize.

Because letters written by attorneys may be called into court as evidence, it is important that each letter begin with a notice of

its place in a sequence of correspondence. The date at the top of
the page helps to establish this place. A subject line like the one
below is also useful, not only for putting the letter in the proper
file but also for establishing the context in which the letter is to
be read.

> Re: Cole v. Comptroller
>   In the Court of Appeals of Utah
>   September Term, 1980
>   No. 1275

In a continuing correspondence, the first line may matter-of-
factly acknowledge the last letter in the series:

This is in response to your letter of June 13, 1980.

Summarizing the letter that is being answered makes the context
more explicit and places a letter more securely within that context.
Here, for example, are three first lines that do just that.

This will acknowledge receipt of your letter of June 13, 1980, cataloging further complaints against my client, Reba Murphy.

This letter is in response to your letter of March 8, 1981, in which you
designated those parts of the record that you proposed to include in
a Joint Record Extract.

In response to the allegations contained in your letter of May 11,
1981, I want to report on two business matters involving Michael
Ransom and Mary Clark.

Notice that this last example not only places the letter in context
but also provides a context for what follows by announcing a discussion that will be divided into two parts. This is an example of
what we call the plural noun formula, a device for organizing and
foreshadowing material by introducing it with a sentence that includes a plural noun, preferably one preceded by a number. (It is
in fact the device we used to organize the first part of this chapter,
announcing that these five main principles would be applied to
specific categories of documents.) In each of the examples below,
the number and noun combination makes organizing the body of a

letter easier for the writer, and comprehending it easier for the reader.

> The list of stipulated facts you proposed in your letter of March 18, 1981, is perfectly acceptable to us, with the exception of three items.

> Marcus Milton, whom I represent, has told me of thirteen instances in which you have failed to promote his book in accordance with specific provisions of his contract with your company.

> In accordance with the rules of discovery approved by the Commission, I am hereby requesting that you produce from your files five documents that we consider to be relevant evidence.

Sentences like these enable the reader to predict what will follow: a description of the three unacceptable stipulations, a description of the thirteen violations of the contract, or a description of the five documents requested. When readers can predict what follows, they can comprehend the substance more easily, making it easier for them to cooperate with the writer if they are inclined to do so.

The longer the letter, the more necessary organizational devices like this become. In a short letter of transmittal, the organizational sequence may not be important. As long as the reader is told within a few lines what is being transmitted, what case it has reference to, and what items in the transmitted document require special attention, it makes little difference what sequence is followed. In longer letters, however, sequence is important. Normally the context and purpose of the letter need to be established at the outset and the body of the letter needs to be foreshadowed. In very long letters the organizational techniques we described for use in decisions and formal memoranda should be consulted, with changes made to accommodate the particular situation.

Many attorneys make the mistake of thinking of organization in their writing as a perfectly desirable but optional virtue, like keeping a standing appointment with a hairdresser or clearing one's desk at the end of each workday. They think that the problems in their writing, if they concede any at all, are likely to be superficial matters of grammar, punctuation, and style.

In our experience, however, organizational problems in legal writing have by far the more profound effects on the quality of the work. We have seen numerous documents that were flawless in grammar and style, but impossible to understand because they were poorly organized. We have seen documents that were illogical because their authors had failed to understand how organization is closely related to the chain of reasoning that connects facts with law and application.

Good organization, then, is not a cosmetic, applied after the document has been thought through and drafted. Organizing and thinking ought to occur at the same time.

The final form of a document may resemble the models published in form books, or it may, in unusual circumstances, be entirely novel. In either case, the form and the logic should support and reveal each other.

5

Style: A Dancer in Chains

In one of our conferences a few years ago, we were working as gingerly as we could with a judge from Pittsburgh. We went over his work with him carefully, parceling out praise and blame, calling each sentence as we saw it. "Here," we said, "you're writing like a human being, but in this passage you're writing like a judge again."

That was a mistake. The judge, a big man, stood up immediately and announced in the sort of voice that might have traveled down a beam of light from a rift in a cloud, "I write like a judge because by God I *am* a judge."

There was more than defensiveness in his response, and something quite different from arrogance. There was confusion, pain, and misunderstanding, and we have seen it not only in judges but in attorneys and even law students. They have gone to a great deal of trouble to learn what they know, including the language that makes their knowledge seem special and grand. They have been told that good writers use lots of words that are unfamiliar to the illiterate mob, and they have worked to collect a word horde of their own. Then we came along and told them that it was all a big mistake—that they ought to learn to write so that any cabbie could make sense of their work. And we were foolish enough to be surprised by their resistance. We thought we were taking off the chains that kept their prose from dancing; they reacted as if we had removed their robes, their pin-striped vests, and heaven knows what else. This, therefore, is a chapter for ambitious attorneys, those who take pride in what they write and who would like to be remembered for the quality of their style.

The first step is to choose the right models. Do not assume that everything printed in lawbooks and legal journals is well written and worthy of imitation; on the contrary, take it on faith that most published legal writing is hack work, utterly without distinction. Look instead to those few members of the law profession whom everybody, lawyers and nonlawyers alike, admires for their style. Notice what Holmes, Cardozo, and Hand do in their writing. Equally important, notice what they do not do.

Here, for example, is a passage by Holmes that we found at a glance in his *Collected Legal Papers*:[1]

> The duty to keep a contract at common law means a prediction that you must pay damages if you do not keep it—and nothing else. If you commit a tort, you are liable to pay a compensatory sum. If you commit a contract, you are liable to pay a compensatory sum unless the promised event comes to pass, and that is all the difference. But such a mode of looking at the matter stinks in the nostrils of those who think it advantageous to get as much ethics into the law as they can.

The same lucidity characterizes the prose of Cardozo, as this passage shows:

> The defendant says that we must stop, in following the chain of causes, when action ceases to be "instinctive." By this is meant, it seems, that rescue is at the peril of the rescuer, unless spontaneous and immediate. If there has been time to deliberate, if impulse has given way to judgment, one cause, it is said, has spent its force, and another has intervened.[2]

For the unambitious lawyer, of course, the elegance and grace of passages like these are turned into a defense of their own pedestrian prose: what is suitable for titans like Holmes and Cardozo, they argue, is hardly appropriate for ordinary laws, contracts, wills, judgments, pleadings, and memoranda. We agree, at least in part. To imitate the rhetorical power of great jurists when ordinary prose is called for would be like pulling a plow with a racehorse. Yet these same passages have another quality that every legal document should have, even the most ordinary. They are all easy to read. They are free from the stylistic ballast that burdens ordinary legal prose, making it dull and sluggish even for readers who have an interest in its substance.

What makes good legal writing good? Partly, of course, the genius of the writers—and that cannot be learned or taught. But partly, too, it requires simple matters of craft, identifiable techniques that can be learned by any willing apprentice with a talent for the trade. These techniques include choosing the right words, using standard tropes like metaphor and irony without allowing them to get out of hand, using as few words as are necessary to express a given idea, and learning to construct sentences with rhythm and grace regardless of their length.

Choosing the right word does not mean avoiding legal terminology or unusual words. The passage from Holmes quoted above has several words and phrases peculiar to the legal profession: *contract, common law, damages, tort, liable,* and the like. The passage from Cardozo has several phrases that no one, not even Cardozo, would be likely to utter spontaneously over a cup of coffee or a cocktail glass, phrases like "rescue is at the peril of the rescuer," and "one cause . . . has spent its force, and another has intervened." There *is* something special about his language, something distinctive from what we ordinarily write and speak.

What makes these choices right, however, is that, in Holmes' case, there is no plainer way to say what he must say; and in Cardozo's case, the style seems so tightly bound to the ideas that we would find it hard to express them in any other words. To be right, special words or phrases must either be inevitable or seem that way. As Horace, the Roman poet, put it, in good art, the technique is not allowed to call attention to itself. When writing stands out from the page inappropriately—that is, when the reader is suddenly aware that the writer is trying hard to make an impression —the artifice, the technique, is no longer concealed as Horace says it should be, and the result is a "purple patch," like this one we found in a Wisconsin divorce action: "Eliciting the value and whereabouts of assets from the plaintiff was akin to trying to pull molasses outdoors in Green Bay in the month of January." The comparison is graphic, we concede, and no doubt accurate; but it calls as much attention to itself as to the passive aggression it was intended to describe.

The same author, not many pages later, joined three metaphors together in this improbable medley:

> On the other side of the coin, the experts on limited alimony point out that a man should be entitled to enjoy his golden age years based on his social security, medicare, and possible pension without the anchor of alimony being hung around his neck for the rest of his life.

In legal writing, metaphor has a place: it can be used to explain, or even to argue, but never merely to decorate. A good example is the metaphor Holmes used to defend his loose construction of the law: "The machinery of government would not work if it were not allowed a little play in its joints."[3] Here the metaphor does not decorate the argument; it is the argument. Metaphors are never completely neutral and explanatory. They always give a phrase an emotional charge, positive or negative, stirring or challenging the reader to feel good or bad about what is being said. Holmes' metaphor makes us feel good about his ignoring the letter of the law, because we feel good about machinery that works.

In addition to metaphor, any of the other traditional ways of heightening language stirs the emotions. It is not easy to resist Cardozo's indignation when he writes a phrase such as "The criminal is to go free because the constable has blundered."[4] The same idea could have been expressed much more forgettably without the balance, alliteration, and chiasmus (the crisscrossing effect of criminal/constable, go free/blundered). Cardozo could have said, "The defendant is to be acquitted because the arresting officer made a mistake." Few people would have noticed, and hardly anyone would have been aroused.

Charged language gives great pleasure to people who agree in advance with what is being said, and who therefore like to see it expressed eloquently. Charged language can also sway the opinion of those who are not firmly committed to either side of the issue being discussed. But charged language has one serious disadvantage: it has an equal but opposite effect on those who do not agree with what it says, sometimes even a bitter effect. Here, for example, is an excerpt from Chief Justice Warren Burger's dissent in a criminal case where the issue was whether the exclusionary rule should have kept critical evidence out of a murder trial.[5] The facts of the crime were ghastly, but the majority opinion held that improper police procedures precluded the admission of certain incriminating statements made by the defendant to public officers. Chief Justice Burger wrote a biting dissent that read more like an editorial polemic than a deliberative judicial opinion. Burger called the majority opinion a "remarkable result," and "astonishing conclusion," and warned against "knee-jerk suppression of relevant and reliable evidence." Here are the opening words of his dissent:

> The result in this case ought to be intolerable in any society which purports to call itself an organized society. It continues the Court— by the narrowest margin—on the much-criticized course of punishing the public for the mistakes and misdeeds of law enforcement officers, instead of punishing the officer directly, if in fact he is guilty of wrongdoing. It mechanically and blindly keeps reliable evidence from juries whether the claimed constitutional violation involves gross police misconduct or honest human error.
>
> Williams is guilty of the savage murder of a small child; no member of the Court contends he is not. While in custody, and after no fewer than *five* warnings of his rights to silence and to counsel, he led police to the concealed body of his victim. The Court concedes Williams was not threatened or coerced and that he spoke and acted voluntarily and with full awareness of his constitutional rights. In the face of all this, the Court now holds that because Williams was prompted by the detective's statement—not interrogation but a statement—the jury must not be told how the police found the body.
>
> Today's holding fulfills Judge (later Mr. Justice) Cardozo's grim prophecy that someday some court might carry the exclusionary rule to the absurd extent that its operative effect would exclude evidence relating to the body of a murder victim because of the means by which it was found. In so ruling the Court regresses to playing a grisly game of "hide and seek," once more exalting the sporting theory of criminal justice which has been experiencing a decline in our jurisprudence. With Justices WHITE, BLACKMUN, and REHNQUIST, I categorically reject the remarkable notion that the police in this case were guilty of unconstitutional misconduct, or any conduct justifying the bizarre result reached by the Court. Apart from a brief comment on the merits, however, I wish to focus on the irrationality of applying the increasingly discredited exclusionary rule to this case.[6]

This is powerful writing. The Supreme Court is the court of last resort, so there is an editorial aspect to its decisions. There is no one left to persuade after this Court rules, except the public and posterity. But what is the likely effect of Chief Justice Burger's strong words on readers who do not share his views about constitutional law and police investigative techniques? No doubt those who shared his views found his charged language a rallying cry. But because the words are so charged, the opinion was likely to cause resentment in those who disagreed, and to polarize differences. Attorneys and judges who are inclined to wax eloquent from time to time should bear this lesson in mind. A reader who does not agree with you is more likely to be offended than persuaded by rhetorical bombast.

Irony can be a delightful form of charged language, provided the reader is sympathetic with the writer's point of view, and provided the litigants do not feel that they are being trifled with. As an example, consider this passage by Lord Cooper of Culross, in *Macleod* v. *Mackenzie,* in which inspectors for Scotland's Price Regulation Committee had fined a village merchant sixty pounds for some sixpence of violations. In mock heroic style, Lord Cooper begins his judgment as if he were Walter Scott beginning a romance:

> In the heart of the Island of Lewis near the head of Loch Erisort there is a clachan called Balallan, in which the complainer keeps the local store, selling articles of clothing, provisions and general merchandise. He also acts as merchant for the local Harris tweed, and he works a croft, and at certain times of the year, particularly in the spring and summer, he also works at cutting, weathering and ingathering peats. His must be a full life, for his activities touch current regulations at countless points. In May 1946 there penetrated into Balallan from Inverness two inspectors of the Price Regulation Committee. . . .[7]

The effect is playful, but not frivolous. The grandiose style is part of the proof that the penalty, too, was disproportionate to the crime.

A similar point is made by the Canadian Mr. Justice Dysart in *Mitchell* v. *Martin and Rose,* wherein the zealous Martin and Rose sentenced the hapless Ms. Mitchell, without the benefit of trial, to six months' safekeeping in a Salvation Army house.

> The plaintiff on her part is described as an infant—being of the tender age of twenty years. Intermittently, she was employed in

Winnipeg, but at the time of which we speak, August 1923, she had managed to "cull her out a holiday" and pay a visit of some days' duration to a friend of hers, in his summer tent on the east bank of the Red River, within the domain of the defendants' jurisdiction.

Upon that occasion and in and about that tent "there were sounds of revelry by night" [Byron, *Childe Harold's Pilgrimage*, canto III, stanza 21]. From the reports which reached the attentive ear of Chief Rose, and which by him have been transmitted to us, we are led to understand that the revelries were indulged in by several persons, male and female; that these bacchanalian revellers frequently burst forth into nocturnal song that filled the great spaces of the night with sounds that echoed far and wide; and that they interspersed their choral offerings by shouts and shrieks that "nightly rent the midnight air."

To the watchful sleepers on the opposite bank of the Red, the nights grew hideous. . . .[8]

It would be misleading for us to suggest that these are examples of the sort of style attorneys should strive for in their routine work. Of course it isn't. What they should strive for, however, is a style that is simple, clean, and direct. Even those dreary clauses in standard contractural and statutory language can be expressed, certainly not elegantly, but at least adequately, in plain style.

The first rule for writing plain style is to be concise. Being concise does not necessarily mean writing short sentences only. It means that in every sentence, short or long, each word has to earn its right to be there, usually by expressing something essential to the meaning, but often by adding some touch of rhythm or grace or emphasis that would be absent if the word was removed.

Wordiness is to a writer what obesity is to a runner. A lawyer participating in one of our seminars, for example, described a residence in these thirty-one words:

This house is a two-story home with the first floor containing a living room, dining room, kitchen, family room and half bath. The second floor has four bedrooms and two baths.

The same information could have been expressed in twenty-four words:

This house has a living room, dining room, kitchen, family room, and half bath on the first floor, with four bedrooms and two baths on the second.

Another lawyer took these twenty-three words to explain an issue raised on appeal:

> Hopgood again attacks the instructions, saying that the trial judge erred in failing to instruct the jury specifically on the question of identity.

With a little effort, six words could have been eliminated:

> Hopgood argues that the trial judge failed to instruct the jury on the question of identity.

Good writers are word misers. They do not say "remanded back" or "referred back," since the meaning of "back" is included in the words preceding them. A good writer would never complain, as an OSAHRC judge once did, that "the rail was not *sufficiently* strong *enough* to protect the workers" (emphasis added). One of these two words would have been sufficient.

One motive for wordiness—at least among judges—is the desire to wield authority with modesty. This, we presume, was why a judge we know wrote: "By reason of the foregoing, I am of the opinion that I am justified in finding that there was negligence on the part of the defendant"—a sentence charming in its humility, but nevertheless as disquieting as the call of a tennis linesman who would shout from his perch, "I believe that I am justified in thinking that your serve was a bit wide of the mark." For the sake of the game, linesmen shout "Fault!" without equivocation if the ball looks out, and judges should write "I find the defendant negligent" if that is what they have decided, despite inevitable misgivings, to find.

Another motive behind legal prolixity is the desire to remove every possible ambiguity from legal documents. No one can gainsay that objective. Unfortunately, every text, no matter how carefully constructed, is inherently ambiguous. We always depend upon a reasonable reader to make a reasonable interpretation, supplementing from context and common sense where necessary. Sometimes the addition of details to prevent ambiguity does little more than delay the reader; sometimes, indeed, the extra baggage *creates* new ambiguities. We were amused, for example, by the Canadian judge who wrote that interest on a promissory note was due from "24th day of October, 1980, A.D. until judgment." He was worried, no doubt, that without the A.D. someone would have computed the interest for four thousand years. Instead of clarifying the sentence, however, it could be argued that "A.D." puts the note in such a grand historical perspective that the "judgment" should be taken to mean not the date on which this document was signed, but that final day of the world's history when all other reckonings will take place.

The same judge wrote that interest would be computed at "15% (percent) per annum," when in fact either the term "percent" or the universally recognized symbol would have conveyed the message.

Attorneys also have the habit of spelling out numbers next to the usual Arabic symbols for them, as in "six (6) months in jail" or "the sum of thirty-two (32) dollars." This mannerism had a purpose when all documents were handwritten, as personal checks still are: if one expression of the amount is ambiguous, the other will frequently remove the doubt. In typed and printed documents, however, the repetition of these figures serves no useful purpose.

Two words saved here, four words saved there—these may seem petty enough at first. But the savings add up. Four words trimmed from a twenty-word sentence is a savings of 20 percent. If 20 percent of a twenty-page document could be eliminated, four pages would be saved, and in all likelihood the reader would have a better chance of understanding the sixteen that remain. Once attorneys become sensitive to the inefficiency of their usual style, they often trim far more than 20 percent from what they write. An administrative trial judge came to a seminar of ours with the paragraph that is printed on the left below; when he was asked to prune the words he considered, on reflection, to be unnecessary, he produced the paragraph on the right.

The Secretary necessarily assumes in alleging the violation that there were asbestos fibers present as defined without attempting to offer any proof that the asbestos fibers were "released" in a manner as set forth in the standard. There is no evidence that the process of installing the sheets as reflected in the record caused asbestos fibers

The Secretary assumes that asbestos fibers were "released" in a manner prohibited by the standard. There is no evidence in the record that the process of installing the sheets caused asbestos fibers in them to be released. The Secretary's contention that the Standard is violated when an employer allows his employees to come in

to be "released." It is also contended that the standard has been violated when an employer allows his employees to come in contact with asbestos, the sheets in this case, without monitoring. This is clearly an unreasonable interpretation of the standard because of the vague nature of its application.

contact with asbestos without monitoring is an unreasonable interpretation of the standard.

The column on the left has 106 words. The column on the right has 66—a reduction of nearly 40 percent. But the numbers do not tell the whole story. The important point here is that the column on the right is much easier to read than the column on the left.

Here is another example, this one written and revised by an attorney in the Federal Trade Commission:

Moreover, respondent is not without resources to develop much of the information which it now seeks from the Commission's files. As one of the largest automotive companies in the world, it must have in its possession or available to it whatever data exist regarding the subject matter of much of the discovery requested here, such as fuel economy procedures, typical mileage obtainable under ordinary driving conditions, and the effect upon fuel economy of driving speed, road surface, grade, weather conditions and other factors.

Some of the requested documents are on the public record. The others duplicate material that the respondent, one of the world's largest automotive companies, must have already.

Was essential information lost in this reduction? Not really, according to the author. What was trimmed was covered elsewhere in the text; not repeating it here made the attorney's point clearer than it had been when the paragraph was loaded with information the reader already knew.

The advice to write concisely should not be confused with the notion that good writers write short sentences. In fact good writers

are not at all afraid of long sentences. Indeed, one of the distinguishing characteristics of a good writer is the ability to construct a
very long sentence that is nevertheless perfectly intelligible when
read once at a normal speed. Here, for example, is one of our
favorites, a line from a children's book by E. B. White:

> In the loveliest town of all, where the houses were white and high
> and the elm trees were green and higher than the houses, where the
> front yards were wide and pleasant and the back yards were bushy
> and worth finding out about, where the streets sloped down to the
> stream and the stream flowed quietly under the bridge, where the
> lawns ended in orchards and the orchards ended in fields and the fields
> ended in pastures and the pastures climbed the hill and disappeared
> over the top toward the wonderful wide sky, in this loveliest of all
> towns Stuart stopped to get a drink of sarsaparilla.[9]

Sentences like this show the fundamental flaw in so-called
readability tests—for example, the scale developed by Rudolph
Flesch or the "fog index" developed by Robert Gunning—based
on the assumption that big words and long sentences are inherently tougher than little words and short sentences. According to
the Gunning fog index, as we understand it, a reader would need
forty-three years of schooling to handle White's sentence. And on
the Flesch scale, according to our calculations, White's sentence
would score minus 10.9 in readability—even lower than selections
from the *IRS Code*, which have been scored at minus 6. On the
Flesch scale, lower scores mean less readability. The *New York
Daily News* has been scored at plus 60, the *Reader's Digest* at 65,
and the *Atlantic* at 57. So what are we to make of children who
seem not only to understand *Stuart Little* but even to enjoy it,
although they find the *IRS Code*, and sometimes the *Atlantic*,
rather tough going? Does this mean that Gunning and Flesch are
wrong?

Well, yes and no. Gunning and Flesch would probably point out
that White's sentence is atypical, and that over a longer stretch of
prose their scales would yield more credible results. But that defense
misses our point, which is that the tests are flawed in their basic
assumptions. Long words, after all, are not necessarily more difficult than short words; "quietly," in White's sentence, is probably

no more difficult than "elm" for most people, even though "quietly" has three times as many syllables. And "sarsaparilla," for which the dictionary records several pronunciations, is probably no more difficult for people who pronounce it in five syllables than it is for those who pronounce it in three. Nor, it would seem, does the length of the sentence make it more difficult to understand than, say, a much shorter sentence that we found in a military court record: "Final findings that refer to a draft finding with no comment on comment sheet should be used as the final reply." What scholars find objectionable, therefore, in these readability tests is that the theory upon which the formulas are based is unsupportable. It is easy to find or to construct counterexamples—long sentences that are readable and short sentences that are unreadable despite their ratings on these scales.

What scholars find frustrating, however, is that the formulas seem to work anyway. When writers are forced to use short words and short sentences, they usually abandon the jargon and tangled syntax that make legal and technical writing difficult to read. The formulas do have a salutary effect, not because they are scientifically valid (they are in fact marvelous pieces of pseudo-science), but because they enforce the common-sense principle that people who don't know how to write long sentences ought to stick to short ones. Or to put it another way, if you write like Zerna Sharp ("See Dick run"), more people will understand you.

What the formulas do not allow for, however, is a legitimate expansiveness of style as it is practiced by recognized writers. They inhibit the construction of sentences like E. B. White's (quoted above) or like this one from Earl Warren's memoirs, which is very much like White's sentence in structure:

> With his popularity, if Eisenhower had said that black children were still being discriminated against long after the adoption of the Thirteenth, Fourteenth, and Fifteenth Amendments, that the Supreme Court of the land had now declared it unconstitutional to continue such cruel practices, and that it should be the duty of every good citizen to help rectify more than eighty years of wrongdoing by honoring that decision—if he had said something to this effect, I think we would have been relieved of many of the racial problems which have continued to plague us.[10]

This sentence and White's show what common sense might have told us anyway: that the difference between a good stylist and a bad one is not a difference between long sentences and short sentences, but a difference in the way in which sentences, short and long, are put together. A good stylist constructs sentences so that, regardless of overall length, information is presented in manageable segments. By "segments" we mean groups of words—not necessarily sentences—that are reasonably complete in themselves. Reading theorists have great difficulty defining a segment precisely: certainly a grammatical sentence is a segment, but those shorter clauses and phrases, enclosed by commas, that make up the bulk of the sentences by White and Warren also seem to be sufficiently complete to be comprehended as segments, and for that reason each entire sentence can be consumed bit by bit.

Warren's and White's sentences are examples of "periodic" sentences. For practical purposes, a periodic sentence can be defined as a sentence in which no punctuation mark or conjunction that could be replaced by a period occurs until the very end. Periodic sentences were popular in classical prose (Cicero used them to great advantage) and in Victorian prose (Cardinal Newman was fond of them), and they appear occasionally even in modern prose. Periodic sentences make demands of both readers and writers. They demand that readers remember the information at the beginning of the sentence for a long time before the predicate comes along to give that information its significance. They demand that the writers set out their information in neat parallel rows (notice the three parallel "that" clauses in Warren's sentence, and the four parallel "where" clauses in White's sentence, with perfect balance within each "where" clause), and if necessary, they remind the reader of what might have been forgotten (notice Warren's repetition of the initial "if" clause near the end, and White's reiteration of "loveliest of all towns"). Good periodic sentences take more planning than ordinary sentences, and therefore more time to write. And because they are formal and dramatic, they should be reserved for formal and dramatic situations—not laws and contracts, but decisions and briefs.

Periodic sentences should be distinguished from other long sentences in which the possibility of a period is delayed, but not gracefully, and to no good effect, like this one, composed by a federal judge who should remain anonymous:

The Government's concern lest the Act be held to be a regulation of production or consumption rather than of marketing is attributable to a few dicta and decisions of this Court which might be understood to lay it down that activities such as "production," "manufacturing," and "mining," are strictly local and, except in special circumstances which are not present here, cannot be regulated under the commerce power because their effects upon interstate commerce are, as a matter of law, only indirect.

One difference between Warren's and White's long sentences and tedious sentences like this one is that Warren's and White's are constructed so that information is presented to the reader in discrete phrases or segments. In this example, however, the first phrase—that is, the first group of words that is either a sentence in itself or a self-contained part of a sentence—is fifty words long, from the beginning to "local," which is where a period might be placed.

For a long sentence to qualify as a periodic sentence, three essential ingredients are required: neat parallelism toward the beginning with information divided into relatively short phrases; a climax or anticlimax worth waiting for at the end; and a rhetorical situation in which the heightened style is appropriate. Our example by the federal judge lacks all three ingredients.

Another kind of long sentence good stylists are fond of is the cumulative sentence. Cumulative sentences are the exact opposite of periodic sentences in that instead of delaying the possibility of a period, they arrive at that possibility fairly early, but drop a comma there and keep on going, adding information in short phrases usually separated by commas. E. B. White is also a master of the cumulative sentence, as he shows in this description of the dachshund who paid regular calls on White's dying pig:

> You could see him down there at all hours, his white face parting the grass along the fence as he wobbled and stumbled about, his stethoscope dangling—a happy quack, writing his villainous prescriptions and grinning his corrosive grin.[11]

Notice that the first comma could have been replaced by a period —after "hours." This means that the first phrase has only nine words—certainly easy enough for most readers to manage. Other marks of punctuation that could be replaced by periods occur after "about," "dangling," and "quack," so that before the period after "grin" the reader has lots of occasions to stop and digest the information being presented bit by bit.

There is plenty of room for sentences of this type in legal writing. Here is an example from a nineteenth-century piece published by Mr. Justice James Stephen in the *Cornhill Magazine*:

> The judge looks at the prisoner for a few moments, makes him a little speech, and pronounces his sentence, often with a good deal of solemnity, but apparently with singularly little principle.[12]

In good writing, the vast majority of sentences are neither cumulative nor periodic, but are made up of some of the characteristics of each, short and long mixed together in a pleasing rhythm, with chunks or discrete units set off by commas forming a second rhythm within the sentences. Carl Sagan is generally regarded as a good stylist. Notice the variety of sentence length in this passage from *The Dragons of Eden*. More important, notice the internal rhythm established by the relatively short phrases within the sentences:

> Yet we are able to date events in the remote past. Geological stratification and radioactive dating provide information on archaeological, paleontological and geological events; and astrophysical theory provides data on the ages of planetary surfaces, stars, and the Milky Way Galaxy, as well as an estimate of the time that has elapsed since that extraordinary event called the Big Bang—an explosion that involved all of the matter and energy in the present universe. The Big Bang may be the beginning of the universe, or it may be a discontinuity in which information about the earlier history of the universe was destroyed. But it is certainly the earliest event about which we have any record.[13]

There is no magic formula for devising readable prose, but note that in the best legal writing, the same sort of rhythm—the same alternation between long and short sentences, rich with interior pauses—occurs. Here, for example, is a famous passage by Supreme Court Justice Brandeis:

> In a government of laws, existence of the government will be imperiled if it fails to observe the law scrupulously. Our Government is

the potent, the omnipresent teacher. For good or for ill, it teaches the whole people by its example. Crime is contagious. If the Government becomes a lawbreaker, it breeds contempt for law; it invites every man to become a law unto himself; it invites anarchy. To declare that in the administration of the criminal law the end justifies the means —to declare that the Government may commit crimes in order to secure the conviction of a private criminal—would bring terrible retribution. Against that pernicious doctrine this Court should resolutely set its face.[14]

Like the passage from *The Dragons of Eden,* this passage has no simpleminded commitment to long sentences or short sentences. It has a variety of sentence length, ranging from those pithy three words "Crime is contagious," which express the heart of the matter, to the dramatic thirty-seven-word periodic sentence ending in "terrible retribution." But again, as in Sagan's passage, the interior rhythm of the sentences—marked by those pauses that give the reader a chance to digest information—is richly varied. The phrases range in size from three words to eighteen. The relative brevity of these phrases makes the passage readable; the frequency and irregularity of the pauses create a pleasant rhythm. As this example shows, there is nothing wrong with legal writing that is pleasant as well as accurate. Lawyers in fact would do well to follow the advice of Horace, the Roman poet, who taught that "mixing sweetness in with practicality is the best way to get your point across" (*omne tulit punctum*). It certainly worked for Brandeis.

But will it work for ordinary mortals at the bar? Of course it will. Here for example is a sentence written by an anonymous student of ours who was working at the time as a correctional official:

Defendant and two others, all armed with pistols, entered the premises of Phil Gottlieb, fur manufacturer, and stole a total of $100,000 in mink coats and skins.

This is a lovely sentence, both sweet and practical. It contains a great deal of actual information, but the information is parceled out in neat phrases. It reads well aloud. It is also free from unnecessary jargon and other stylistic flaws.

We often ask students in our seminars to produce rhythmic sentences like these after we have shown them how to do it. Here is a gem produced by Charles D. Nelson, who is working with the Federal Trade Commission:

> Congress passed this law in 1978 to end the revolving-door syndrome, the ever-increasing flow of federal executives, technicians, and attorneys from federal agencies to the industries the agencies regulate or do business with.

And here is another by Larry Weiner, a lawyer who was at the time working for the Occupational Safety and Health Review Commission:

> At trial the truth emerges only as the evidence portrays it, often only partially, too often not at all.

We wish we could take the credit for making writers of these attorneys, but obviously they had brought considerable talent with them when they came to class. So did the Honorable William R. Dunn, a judge in Covington, Kentucky, who dismissed a briefcase full of frivolous defenses against a malpractice charge with a telling metaphor—"After a winnowing of the various issues and arguments advanced by appellant, there remains but a single issue"—and carved up the rest of the argument with rapier-sharp sentences like these:

> Also, we find no merit in appellant's view that the hours he spent in defending himself on the charges before the bar associations should have been considered in determining the extent of the services rendered. These were on his behalf, not hers, and were properly ignored.

Superior writing is not reserved for the titans alone. With a little talent and a lot of craftsmanship, any lawyer can do it.

In his introduction to *The Language of the Law*,[15] Louis Blom-Cooper argues that it is impossible for a judge to remain at the stylistic level represented by the examples in his collection "for any sustained period of time." He illustrates his point by quoting a magnificent opening and eloquent conclusion of a speech by Lord Macnaghten, and then conceding that "between the two passages cited lie over four thousand words which, while they are caviar to the lawyer, hold nothing but unrelieved tedium for the layman."[16]

If Blom-Cooper's judgment is correct, than the failure is in Lord Macnaghten's style, not in his subject matter. Although some cases may lack broad public interest or dramatic human conflict, every case that comes to the bar is inherently interesting, at least to the litigants themselves if to no one else. Even the most ethereal ratiocinations dividing the spoils in a bankruptcy case or assigning tax liabilities to corporate giants are interesting, certainly to those people who have a stake in the results. Whenever the litigants and other concerned parties are not riveted to every page their attorneys write about their conflicts, then in all likelihood the attorneys have written poorly indeed.

The failure is usually caused by shackling the style with chains that would make any prose grow weary: excessive verbiage, embarrassing metaphors, and tortuous sentence structure. Once these chains are removed, once the attorney discovers that these bonds are not natural in language or useful to the law, legal style can fairly dance across the page.

6

Before and After

Remember those diet ads that showed a massive body juxtaposed with a trim, more attractive one, with "before" and "after" captions? We were reminded of them when a Minnesota trial judge showed us one of his opinions that he had edited during a week-long judicial writing course. Look at the differences between the introduction and conclusion to his opinion, before and after his editing.

<table>
<tr><td align="center">BEFORE</td><td align="center">AFTER</td></tr>
<tr><td>The above-entitled matter came on for hearing before the undersigned on November 8, 1976, pursuant to a motion and notice thereof, duly served and filed, in which the motion petitioner moved the court for an order (1) dismissing the complaint herein, or, (2) in the alternative, for an order remanding the said matter to the hearing examiner for the presentation of such additional evidence as may be necessary.</td><td>This case arose from petitioner's motion for an order (1) dismissing the complaint or, (2) in the alternative, for an order remanding the case to the hearing examiner for the presentation of additional evidence.</td></tr>
</table>

The parties were not present but were represented by counsel, Vance B. Grannis for the petitioner and Erica Jacobson, special assistant attorney general, for respondent. The motion was based upon the affidavit of Vance B. Grannis and upon all the files, records and proceedings. Both parties submitted memoranda in support of their respective positions.

Upon all the files, records and proceedings had and filed in said matter, arguments and memoranda of Counsel and after due consideration of the same,

IT IS ORDERED

1. That petitioner's motion to dismiss the complaint herein be and the same is hereby denied. 2. That petitioner's motion to remand the above-entitled matter to the hearing examiner for presentation of such additional evidence as may be necessary, be and the same is hereby denied.

IT IS ORDERED

1. Petitioner's motion to dismiss the complaint is denied.

2. Petitioner's motion to remand to the hearing examiner is denied.

This example graphically illustrates the virtue of editing legal gobbledygook. The judge deleted nothing substantial from his opinion. His message was clearer as a result of editing.

Imagine the enormous savings in printing and storage costs that would result from cutting all judicial opinions as drastically as this judge pruned his own. The same applies to all legal documents, from straightforward letters or memoranda, to more consequential formal documents—wills, contracts, trusts, varied business agreements—to the most technical pleadings and briefs that lawyers prepare chiefly for each other.

Take, for example, the introductory and attestation clauses commonly used in wills by lawyers who unthinkingly rely on clumsy boilerplate forms. The second version requires half as much space as the first, yet says the same thing and says it more clearly.

I. Introductory Clause

BEFORE	AFTER
I, L.M.D., of the Borough of Manhattan, County, City and State of New York, being of sound and disposing mind and memory and being aware of the uncertainty of this life, and of the natural objects of my bounty, do hereby make, publish and declare this to be my last Will and Testament, hereby revoking any and all other Wills by me heretofore made.	I, L.M.D., a resident of New York City, hereby make this Will and revoke all my prior wills and codicils.

XXV. Attestation Clause

BEFORE	AFTER
The above instrument, consisting of Twenty-One (21) typewritten pages, including the page on which we, the undersigned, have subscribed our names as witnesses, was at the date thereof subscribed, sealed, published and declared by L.M.D., the aforesaid Testatrix, as and for her Last Will and Testament, in the presence of each other, have hereunto subscribed our names as witnesses thereto (the final clause of the Will having been read aloud to us by the aforesaid Testatrix immediately after she had signed the Will, and this clause having been thereupon read aloud in her and our presence and hearing), this _____ day of _____, One Thousand Nine Hundred and Eighty (1980).	This instrument, consisting of Twenty-One (21) typewritten pages, including this page on which we have subscribed our names as witnesses, was today subscribed and declared by L.M.D., the Testatrix, as her Last Will and Testament, executed on March 22, 1980. In her presence and in the presence of each other, we have signed as witness on this _____ day of _____, 1980.

More substantive are the property-disposing provisions of wills, which could be shortened and simplified without risk to clients.

BEFORE	AFTER
All the rest, remainder, and residue of my property, real and personal and wheresoever situated, of which I may die seized or possessed, including lapsed legacies and devices, and including all property over which I shall have a power of appointment, I give, devise, and bequeath absolutely and in fee simple, to my wife, J.C.S.	I give everything else to my wife, J.C.S. If she dies first or at the same time, I give everything else to my daughter, A.C.S.
If my said wife, J.C.S., shall predecease me or if we shall die simultaneously, then and in that event, all the rest, residue and remainder of my property, real and personal, and wheresoever situated, including all property over which I shall have a power of appointment, I give, devise, and bequeath absolutely and in fee simple, to my daughter, A.C.S.	

Consider another relatively simple and commonplace legal document. Here is a release sent to us recently by a Philadelphia attorney as part of a settlement. The names of the parties are changed to protect the innocent.

BEFORE	AFTER
Release	*Release*
KNOW ALL MEN BY THESE PRESENTS, that Ronald Goldfarb for and in consideration of Five Hundred Dollars ($500.00) lawful money of the United States of America in hand paid by the Raymond Corporation, at the delivery hereof, the receipt of which is hereby acknowledged, and other good and valuable consideration,	In return for $500.00 paid to him by the Raymond Corporation, Ronald Goldfarb hereby releases the Raymond Corporation and every person and organization connected with it from all claims arising out of Goldfarb's disputed bill for $2,145.00 dated February 14, 1981.
	Signed and dated.

has remised, released and forever
discharged, and does by these presents for himself, his successors,
executors, administrators, assigns
and heirs of him, release, remise
and forever discharge James Raymond, the Raymond Corporation,
Raymond Research, Raymond &
Raymond, Ltd., Raymond International, the Raymond Group,
and Ray-Mond, Inc., collectively,
the James C. Raymond Company,
their successors and assigns, of
and from all manner of actions,
cause and causes of action, suits,
debts, dues, sums of money, accounts, reckonings, bonds, skills,
contracts, controversies, covenants,
agreements, promises, damages,
awards, claims, demands and judgments, whatsoever in law or in
equity, known or unknown, which
he now has or may hereafter have
against said James C. Raymond,
the Raymond Corporation, Raymond Research, Raymond & Raymond, Ltd., Raymond International, the Raymond Group, and
Ray-Mond, Inc., collectively, the
James C. Raymond Company, its
successors or assigns, for or by
reason or any cause, matter or
saying whatsoever from the beginning of the world to the date of
these presents. Without limiting
in any way the nature or effect of
this general release, Ronald Goldfarb understands and agrees that
this release includes within its
provisions and terms any and all
claims he may now have, may have
had, or may hereafter have arising
out of or in any way connected,

directly or indirectly, with a
$2,145.00 claim submitted by a
bill initially dated February 14,
1981, for alleged service performed
consisting allegedly of a written
proposal for a media services ex-
pansion.
   In WITNESS WHEREOF,
Ronald Goldfarb has caused these
presents to be executed and sealed
this 15th day of April 1981.
Witness_____Signature_____
(SEAL)

One lawyer who was critical of legalese lamented how his colleagues could turn a simple phrase into 286 words without batting
an eye. With a lease requiring the tenant to pay the taxes, he
showed how an imaginative lawyer could state this single fact
interminably:

> all real estate taxes, assessments, water rents and charges, and govern-
> mental impositions, duties and charges of every kind and nature
> whatsoever, extraordinary as well as ordinary and whether now within
> the contemplation of the parties or not, and each and every install-
> ment of each of them which shall or may during the term of this
> lease be charged, laid, levied, assessed or imposed upon, or become a
> lien or liens upon the demised premises or any part thereof, or upon
> any building or appurtenances thereto, or any part thereof, or upon
> any sidewalks or streets in front of or adjoining the demised premises,
> or which may become due and payable with respect thereto, and any
> and all taxes, charged, laid, levied, assessed or imposed in lieu of or
> in addition to the foregoing, under or by virtue of any present or
> future laws, rules, requirements, orders, directions, ordinances or
> regulations of the United States of America, or of the state, county
> or city government or of any other municipal, governmental or lawful
> authority whatsoever. . . .[1]

Irving Kellogg, a Los Angeles lawyer, recently made the case for
using plain English in the everyday documents of law and commerce.[2] Organize your thoughts, keep your writing short and simple,
use the active voice, he said:

My office has used these techniques for some time. The investment in plain English conversion resulted in increased earnings, increased time to do other things, personal creative satisfaction, client compliments about understandability, client referrals, client recognition of the differences between plain English documents and prior counsel's documents, fewer explanation conferences and less redrafting.[3]

On page 109 are Irving Kellogg's examples of traditional parts of a stockholders' buy-sell agreement—before and after he cleaned up their language.

And on pages 110 and 111 is his limited partnership agreement before and after he edited and simplified it.

A few years ago we were asked by a national credit union to simplify its loan agreements, consistent with the numerous legal requirements governing these documents. According to the general manager who hired us, the documents that were being used at the time had been drafted by one attorney and revised by another, but they remained a "real attorney's monster." He was correct. We reread the documents repeatedly—including the form instructions and cover letter that went to each loan candidate—and were still confused and unsure of the message. The documents are too long to reproduce; but the experience was remarkable. If it took a lawyer days to study and comprehend them, how could they make sense to the general public? Remember, these were documents to be used by ordinary citizens. There is no way they could have known what they were agreeing to.

The First National Bank, known as Citibank, the country's second largest bank holding company, is one of the nation's leaders in the plain English movement. Several years ago, it began a process of redesigning and rewording its common consumer agreements—installment loan notes, safe deposit lease agreements, banking agreements, and consumer continuing guaranties. Its work received wide publicity as a major example of how the use of plain English would aid public relations and not hamper the flow of business. On pages 112–113 and 114 are its former promissory note and its new version.

The Citibank forms demonstrate another important point. Along with clear language, clear visual presentation is an important aspect of well-written legal documents, especially complex legislation and regulations.

TABLE IV: PAYMENT OF PURCHASE PRICE

Original

(a) Initial Payment. In the event of the death of Smith or Jones, one-half (½) of the proceeds of life insurance receivable by the Corporation shall be paid in cash (Initial Payment) to the Smith Trust or to the Jones Trust (as the case may be), or to the Estate of the Deceased Stockholder or other transferee of the shares now held in such Trust if his trust has been previously terminated or revoked. The Initial Payment shall be made as soon as the Insurance Proceeds have been received from the Insurance Company, but such Initial Payment shall be paid in any event not later than 180 days after the death of the deceased Stockholder.

Revision

(a) Initial Payment. The Initial Payment for the decedent's shares is one-half (½) of the life insurance proceeds received by the Corporation because of that death. The Corporation shall by check pay the owners of those shares pro-rata, as soon as is reasonable, but in no event later than 6 months after the Stockholder's death.

TABLE V: OBLIGATION TO DELIVER DECEDENT'S SHARES

Original

(c) The Trustee of the Smith Trust or the Trustee of the Jones Trust (as the case may be), or, if such Trust has been revoked or terminated, the legal representative of the Estate of the deceased Stockholder (or such other transferee as may then hold the shares originally transferred to a Trust by the deceased Stockholder) shall deliver the purchased shares of the Corporation to the Secretary of the Corporation properly endorsed and in every other respect prepared for repurchase, concurrently with the Corporation's tender of the Initial Payment for such shares.

Revision 1

(c) The person holding shares subject to this Agreement shall deliver them to the Corporation's Secretary at the same time the Corporation makes the Initial Payment. The shares shall be properly endorsed for transfer.

Revision 2

(c) The person owning shares subject to this Agreement shall (1) properly endorse them for transfer to the Corporation and (2) deliver them to the Corporation's Secretary at the same time the Corporation makes the Initial Payment.

TABLE VI: TERMINATION OF PRIOR AGREEMENT

Original

The parties hereto agree that this is the sole and entire agreement of the parties with respect to the entire subject hereof, and there are no other agreements whether written or oral, which modify or supplement the provisions of this agreement. In this regard, the parties hereto expressly agree that the Stock Purchase Agreement executed by and among Smith, Jones, and the Corporation dated March 5, 1980 is hereby cancelled and terminated. Any and all rights the parties hereto may have had pursuant to the terms and provisions of the March 5, 1980 Stock Purchase Agreement are extinguished.

Revision 1

This is the only agreement among the parties about the Corporation's stock. There are no other agreements. The March 5, 1980 Stock Purchase Agreement is cancelled. All rights the parties may have had under it are cancelled.

Revision 2

This is the only agreement among the parties about the Corporation's stock. The March 5, 1980 Stock Purchase Agreement and all rights under it are cancelled. *Revision of second sentence*: This agreement cancels (1) the March 5, 1980 Stock Purchase Agreement and (2) all rights under it.

TABLE I

AGREEMENT OF LIMITED PARTNERSHIP
OF
PARKWAY SHOPPING CENTER ASSOCIATES, LTD.
A California Limited Partnership

THIS AGREEMENT OF LIMITED PARTNERSHIP (this "Agreement") is made and entered into in the County of Los Angeles, State of California, by and among John Jones (Jones) and Richard Smith (Smith) as the General Partners (collectively, "the General Partner") and the persons signatory hereto determined by the General Partner in its sole and absolute discretion whose names appear in Exhibit A attached hereto and made a part hereof (individually, a or any "Limited Partner", and collectively the "Limited Partners") and is dated for identification purposes only the 1st day of October, 1980.

RECITALS

A. Investment Objectives. The parties hereto for their mutual advantage desire, either alone or in conjunction with others, for investment purposes only to pool their capital and resources in order to acquire, improve, hold, maintain, operate and lease a commercial shopping center, commonly known as the Parkway Shopping Center, comprising approximately Two Hundred Thousand (200,000) square feet of rental space, located in Santa Maria, California, and legally described on Exhibit B attached hereto and made a part hereof (collectively, the "Property") and to engage in any and all business activities related or incidental thereto consistent with the terms and conditions of this Agreement (the "Investment Objectives").

B. The General Partner has acquired the Property in its own name and is willing to transfer all of its rights thereto to the Limited Partnership in exchange for reimbursement of its out-of-pocket costs incurred in connection therewith and its general partnership interest herein.

C. Formation of Limited Partnership. The parties hereto in pursuit of the Investment Objectives desire to form a limited partnership (the "Limited Partnership") under the laws of the State of California.

NOW THEREFORE, the parties hereto do hereby agree as follows:

1. Formation of Limited Partnership.

1.1 Formation. Subject to the provision of Section 2 hereof, the parties hereto do hereby agree:

1.1.1 Uniform Limited Partnership Act. To form the Limited Partnership pursuant to the provisions of the Corporations Code of the State of California (the "Corporations Code") Title 2, Chapter 2, Sections 15501 through 15531, inclusive which sections constitute the Uniform Limited Partnership Act and shall govern the relationship among the parties hereto except as expressly provided to the contrary herein.

1.1.2 Certificate of Limited Partnership. To prepare, execute, file and have recorded a certificate of limited partnership (the "Certificate of Limited Partnership") in the form, substance and manner required by the Corporations Code Section 15502.

1.1.3 Fictitious Business Name Statement. To prepare, execute, file and have published and recorded a fictitious business name statement (the "Fictitious Business Name Statement") in the form, substance and manner required by the Business and Professions Code of the State of California (the "Business and Professions Code") Sections 17900 through 17930, inclusive.

1.1.4 Further Assurances. Take any and all other actions as may from time to time be required under the laws of the State of California to give effect to and continue in good standing the Limited Partnership.

1.2 Name. The name of the Limited Partnership shall be Parkway Shopping Center Associates Ltd.

1.3 Principal Place of Business. The principal place of business of the Limited Partnership shall be 4321 Real Estate Center Building, 695 South Flower Street, Los Angeles, California or such other place or places as the General Partner may from time to time determine in its sole and absolute discretion.

1.4 Purposes. The purpose of the Limited Partnership shall be to pursue the Investment Objectives.

1.5 Term. The term of the Limited Partnership shall commence as of the date of filing and recording of the Certificate of Limited Partnership pursuant to the provisions of Section 1.1.2 hereof and shall continue until dissolved, liquidated and terminated pursuant to the provisions of Section 7.2 hereof.

TABLE II: LIMITED PARTNERSHIP AGREEMENT

Article I: **Facts and Declarations**

    1.1   Date for identification purposes:

    1.2   Name of Partnership: Parkway Shopping Center Associates, Ltd.

    1.3   General Partners: John Jones and Richard Smith, or the survivor of them, 2800 Avenue of the Stars, Los Angeles, California 90067.

    1.4   Limited Partners: See Exhibit A.

    1.5   Address of the Partnership:
4321 Real Estate Center Building
695 S. Flower Street
Los Angeles, California 90060

    1.6   Limited Partners' Capital Investment:
See Exhibit A.

    1.7   Fiscal year of Partnership: Calendar Year

    1.8   Profit or Loss Percentages: See Exhibit A

    1.9   Cash Flow Distributions: See Exhibit B

    1.10   Investment Objectives: The parties join to pool their resources to buy and to operate a commercial shopping center in Santa Maria, California. It is the Parkway Shopping Center. It consists of about 200,000 square feet of rental space. The legal description is in Exhibit B of this agreement. This agreement refers to the shopping center as the Property.

    1.11   Transfer of Property: The General Partners have bought the property in their names. They will transfer their ownership to this partnership in exchange for the partnership reimbursing them for their out-of-pocket costs incurred in all aspects of the purchase.

    1.12   Term of the Partnership: The partnership begins at the time the Certificate of Limited Partnership is recorded and ends under the provisions of paragraph 7.2.

Article II: **Agreement Among the Partners**

    2.1   The General and Limited Partners agree to form this limited partnership under the Uniform Limited Partnership Section of the California Corporations Code. Unless otherwise provided for in this agreement, those Sections govern the partners' relationships.

Article III: **Formation and Administration Obligations of the General Partners.**

    3.1   The General Partners shall do what is needed to:
(1) Record a Certificate of Limited Partnership;
(2) Record a Fictitious Business Name Statement;
(3) Keep the partnership in good standing in California;
(4) In accord with standard real estate accounting practice, keep accurate accounting records of the partnership's transactions on a cash basis.
(5) Deliver to each Limited Partner within 60 days after December 31, a financial report of the partnership's activities for the year ending on that date;
(6) Conduct the partnership business affairs so as to achieve the maximum income and capital appreciation results of the investment objective within their reasonable powers to do so taking into account the usual risks in such an operation.

BEFORE

FIRST NATIONAL CITY BANK
PERSONAL FINANCE DEPARTMENT - NEW YORK
APPLICATION
NUMBER _____

ANNUAL PER-CENTAGE RATE _____ %

$ _____

PROCEEDS TO BORROWER	(1) $	_____
PROPERTY INS. PREMIUM	(2) $	_____
FILING FEE	(3) $	_____
AMOUNT FINANCED (1) + (2) + (3)	(4) $	_____
PREPAID FINANCE CHARGE	(5) $	_____
GROUP CREDIT LIFE INS. PREMIUM	(6) $	_____
FINANCE CHARGE (5) + (6)	(7) $	_____

TOTAL OF PAYMENTS (4) + (7)

FOR VALUE RECEIVED, the undersigned (jointly and severally) hereby promise(s) to pay to FIRST NATIONAL CITY BANK (the "Bank") at its office at 399 Park Avenue, New York, New York 10022 (i) THE SUM OF

_____ ($ _____) (TOTAL OF PAYMENTS)

( ) IN _____ EQUAL CONSECUTIVE MONTHLY INSTALMENTS OF $ _____ EACH ON THE SAME DAY OF EACH MONTH, COMMENCING _____ DAYS FROM THE DATE THE LOAN IS MADE; OR ( ) IN _____ EQUAL CONSECUTIVE WEEKLY INSTALMENTS OF $ _____ EACH ON THE SAME DAY OF EACH WEEK, COMMENCING NOT EARLIER THAN 5 DAYS NOR LATER THAN 45 DAYS FROM THE DATE THE LOAN IS MADE; OR ( ) IN _____ EQUAL CONSECUTIVE BI-WEEKLY INSTALMENTS OF $ _____ EACH, COMMENCING NOT EARLIER THAN 10 DAYS NOR LATER THAN 45 DAYS FROM THE DATE THE LOAN IS MADE, AND ON THE SAME DAY OF EACH SECOND WEEK THEREAFTER; OR ( ) IN _____ EQUAL CONSECUTIVE SEMI-MONTHLY INSTALMENTS OF $ _____ EACH, COMMENCING NOT EARLIER THAN 10 DAYS NOR LATER THAN 45 DAYS FROM THE DATE THE LOAN IS MADE, AND ON THE SAME DAY OF EACH SEMI-MONTHLY PERIOD THEREAFTER, (ii) A FINE COMPUTED AT THE RATE OF 5¢ PER $1 ON ANY INSTALMENT WHICH HAS BECOME DUE AND REMAINED UNPAID FOR A PERIOD IN EXCESS OF 10 DAYS, PROVIDED (A) IF THE PROCEEDS TO THE BORROWER ARE $10,000 OR LESS, NO SUCH FINE SHALL EXCEED $5 AND THE AGGREGATE OF ALL SUCH FINES SHALL NOT EXCEED THE LESSER OF 2% OF THE AMOUNT OF THIS NOTE OR $25, OR (B) IF THE ANNUAL PERCENTAGE RATE STATED ABOVE IS 7.50% OR LESS, THE LIMITATIONS PROVIDED IN (A) SHALL NOT APPLY AND NO SUCH FINE SHALL EXCEED $25 AND THE AGGREGATE OF ALL SUCH FINES SHALL NOT EXCEED 2% OF THE AMOUNT OF THIS NOTE, AND SUCH FINE(S) SHALL BE DEEMED LIQUIDATED DAMAGES OCCASIONED BY THE LATE PAYMENT(S); (iii) IN THE EVENT OF THIS NOTE MATURING, SUBJECT TO AN ALLOWANCE FOR UNEARNED INTEREST ATTRIBUTABLE TO THE MATURED AMOUNT, INTEREST AT A RATE EQUAL TO 1% PER MONTH AND (iv) IF THIS NOTE IS REFERRED TO AN ATTORNEY FOR COLLECTION, A SUM EQUAL TO ALL COSTS AND EXPENSES THEREOF, INCLUDING AN ATTORNEY'S FEE EQUAL TO 15% OF THE AMOUNT OWING ON THIS NOTE AT THE TIME OF SUCH REFERENCE, PLUS NECESSARY COURT COSTS. THE ACCEPTANCE BY THE BANK OF ANY PAYMENT(S) EVEN IF MARKED PAYMENT IN FULL OR SIMILAR WORDING, OR IF MADE AFTER ANY DEFAULT HEREUNDER, SHALL NOT OPERATE TO EXTEND THE TIME OF PAYMENT OF OR TO WAIVE ANY AMOUNT(S) THEN REMAINING UNPAID OR CONSTITUTE A WAIVER OF ANY RIGHTS OF THE BANK HEREUNDER.

IN THE EVENT THIS NOTE IS PREPAID IN FULL OR REFINANCED, THE BORROWER SHALL RECEIVE A REFUND OF THE UNEARNED PORTION OF THE PREPAID FINANCE CHARGE COMPUTED IN ACCORDANCE WITH THE RULE OF 78 (THE "SUM OF THE DIGITS" METHOD), PROVIDED THAT THE BANK MAY RETAIN A MINIMUM FINANCE CHARGE OF $10, WHETHER OR NOT EARNED, AND, EXCEPT IN THE CASE OF A REFINANCING, NO REFUND SHALL BE MADE IF IT AMOUNTS TO LESS THAN $1. IN ADDITION, UPON ANY SUCH PREPAYMENT OR REFINANCING, THE BORROWER SHALL RECEIVE A REFUND OF THE CHARGE, IF ANY, FOR GROUP CREDIT LIFE INSURANCE INCLUDED IN THE LOAN EQUAL TO THE UNEARNED PORTION OF THE PREMIUM PAID OR PAYABLE BY THE HOLDER OF THE OBLIGATION (COMPUTED IN ACCORDANCE WITH THE RULE OF 78), PROVIDED THAT NO REFUND SHALL BE MADE OF AMOUNTS LESS THAN $1.

AS COLLATERAL SECURITY FOR THE PAYMENT OF THE INDEBTEDNESS OF THE UNDERSIGNED HEREUNDER AND ALL OTHER INDEBTEDNESS OR LIABILITIES OF THE UNDERSIGNED TO THE BANK, WHETHER JOINT, SEVERAL, ABSOLUTE, CONTINGENT, SECURED, UNSECURED, MATURED OR UNMATURED, UNDER ANY PRESENT OR FUTURE NOTE OR CONTRACT OR AGREEMENT WITH THE BANK (ALL SUCH INDEBTEDNESS AND LIABILITIES BEING HEREINAFTER COLLECTIVELY CALLED THE "OBLIGATIONS"), THE BANK SHALL HAVE, AND IS HEREBY GRANTED, A SECURITY INTEREST IN AND TO (a) ALL MONIES, SECURITIES AND OTHER PROPERTY OF THE UNDERSIGNED NOW OR HEREAFTER ON DEPOSIT WITH OR COMING TO THE POSSESSION OR UNDER THE CONTROL OF THE BANK, WHETHER HELD FOR SAFEKEEPING, COLLECTION, TRANSMISSION OR OTHERWISE OR AS CUSTODIAN, INCLUDING THE PROCEEDS THEREOF, AND ANY AND ALL CLAIMS OF THE UNDERSIGNED AGAINST THE BANK, WHETHER NOW OR HEREAFTER EXISTING, AND (b) THE FOLLOWING DESCRIBED PERSONAL PROPERTY (ALL SUCH MONIES, SECURITIES, PROPERTY, PROCEEDS, CLAIMS AND PERSONAL PROPERTY BEING HEREINAFTER COLLECTIVELY CALLED THE "COLLATERAL"): ( ) Motor Vehicle ( ) Boat ( ) Stocks, ( ) Bonds, ( ) Savings, and/or ____

SEE CUSTOMER'S COPY OF SECURITY AGREEMENT(S) OR COLLATERAL RECEIPT(S) RELATIVE TO THIS LOAN FOR FULL DESCRIPTION.

IF THIS NOTE IS SECURED BY A MOTOR VEHICLE, BOAT OR AIRCRAFT, PROPERTY INSURANCE ON THE COLLATERAL IS REQUIRED, AND THE BORROWER MAY OBTAIN THE SAME THROUGH A PERSON OF HIS OWN CHOICE.

IF THIS NOTE IS NOT FULLY SECURED BY THE COLLATERAL SPECIFIED ABOVE, AS FURTHER SECURITY FOR THE PAYMENT OF THIS NOTE, THE BANK HAS TAKEN AN ASSIGNMENT OF 10% OF THE UNDERSIGNED BORROWER'S WAGES IN ACCORDANCE WITH THE WAGE ASSIGNMENT ATTACHED TO THIS NOTE.

In the event of default in payment of this or any other Obligation or the performance or observance of any term or covenant contained herein or in any note or other contract or agreement evidencing or relating to any Obligation or any Collateral on the Borrower's part to be performed or observed; or the undersigned Borrower shall die; or any of the undersigned become insolvent or make an assignment for the benefit of creditors; or a petition shall be filed by or against any of the undersigned under any provision of the Bankruptcy Act; or any money, securities or property of the undersigned now or hereafter on deposit with or in the possession or under the control of the Bank shall be attached or become subject to distraint proceedings or any order or process of any court; or the Bank shall deem itself to be insecure, then and in any such event, the Bank shall have the right (at its option), without demand or notice of any kind, to declare all or any part of the Obligations to be immediately due and payable, whereupon such Obligations shall become and be immediately due and payable, and the Bank shall have the right to exercise all the rights and remedies available to a secured party upon default under the Uniform Commercial Code (the "Code") in effect in New York at the time, and such other rights and remedies as may otherwise be provided by law. Each of the undersigned agrees (for purposes of the "Code") that written notice of any proposed sale of, or of the Bank's election to retain, Collateral mailed to the undersigned Borrower (who is hereby appointed agent of each of the undersigned for such purpose) by first class mail, postage prepaid, at the address of the undersigned Borrower indicated below three business days prior to such sale or election shall be deemed reasonable notification thereof. The remedies of the Bank hereunder are cumulative and may be exercised concurrently or separately. If any provision of this paragraph shall conflict with any remedial provision contained in any security agreement or collateral receipt covering any Collateral, the provisions of such security agreement or collateral receipt shall control.

Acceptance by the Bank of payments in arrears shall not constitute a waiver of or otherwise affect any acceleration of payment hereunder or other right or remedy exercisable hereunder. No failure or delay on the part of the Bank in exercising, and no failure to file or otherwise perfect or enforce the Bank's security interest in or with respect to any Collateral, shall operate as a waiver of any right or remedy hereunder or release any of the undersigned, and the Obligations of the undersigned may be extended or waived by the Bank, any contract or other agreement evidencing or relating to any Obligation or any Collateral may be amended and any Collateral exchanged, surrendered or otherwise dealt with in accordance with any agreement relative thereto, all without affecting the liability of any of the undersigned. In any litigation (whether or not arising out of or related to any Obligation or Collateral or other matter connected herewith) in which the Bank and any of the undersigned may be adverse parties, the Bank and each such undersigned hereby waives their respective right to demand trial by jury and, additionally, each such undersigned waives his right to interpose in any such litigation any counterclaim of any nature or description which he may have against the Bank. In addition, the Bank shall not be deemed to have obtained knowledge of any fact or notice with respect to any matter relating to this note or any Collateral unless contained in a written notice mailed, postage prepaid, or personally delivered to the Personal Finance Department of the Bank at its address set forth above. Each of the undersigned, by his signature hereto, hereby waives presentation for payment, demand, notice of non-payment, protest and notice of protest with respect to the indebtedness evidenced by this note, and each such undersigned hereby agrees that this note shall be deemed to have been made under and shall be construed in accordance with the laws of the State of New York.

Each of the undersigned hereby authorizes the Bank to date this note as of the day the loan evidenced hereby is made, to correct patent errors herein and, at its option, to cause the signatures of one or more co-makers to be added without notice to any prior obligor.

RECEIPT OF A COPY OF THIS NOTE, APPROPRIATELY FILLED IN, IS HEREBY ACKNOWLEDGED BY THE BORROWER

FULL SIGNATURE   COMPLETE ADDRESSES

BORROWER _____

WIFE OR HUSBAND OF BORROWER AS CO-MAKER _____

CO-MAKER _____

CO-MAKER _____

ASSIGNMENT OF WAGES, SALARY, COMMISSIONS OR OTHER COMPENSATION FOR SERVICES

This Assignment is executed as security for, or as a manner or method of repayment of, money advanced by a bank, trust company or credit union doing business in New York.

To: **FIRST NATIONAL CITY BANK — AS ASSIGNEE**
PERSONAL FINANCE DEPARTMENT
810 SEVENTH AVENUE
NEW YORK, NEW YORK 10019

Date _____ , 19 ____

I, the undersigned, being the "Borrower" indicated on the promissory note which appears above, in consideration of your making the loan evidenced by said note, do hereby assign to you, as collateral security for the payment of the indebtedness evidenced thereby, any and all monies which may hereafter become due or owing to me as salary, wages, commissions or other compensation for services from any present or future employer of mine (herein referred to as my "Employer"), to the extent of an amount equal to 10%, thereof, computed at the time when such salary, wage(s), commission(s), or other compensation is (are) payable, and you are hereby authorized to apply the same, as and when received by you, to the satisfaction of all such indebtedness as shall then be due and owing by the undersigned on account of said note until all such indebtedness shall be fully paid.

I hereby authorize my Employer to give full force and effect hereto, he being hereby released and discharged from any and all liability to me for or on account of any and all monies which may be paid you hereunder.

I hereby acknowledge receipt of a copy hereof.

THIS IS AN ASSIGNMENT OF WAGES, SALARY, COMMISSIONS OR OTHER COMPENSATION FOR SERVICES.

SIGNATURE OF ASSIGNOR   SIGN FULL NAME _____

(SIGNATURE OF COMPLETE NAME OF ASSIGNOR)

NOTICE OF PROPOSED GROUP INSURANCE

Credit life insurance on the life of the "Borrower" obligated under the Note on the reverse side hereof may be taken out by the Bank under a group life insurance policy issued to the Bank by The Prudential Insurance Company of America, having its home office in Newark, New Jersey. Such insurance, if effected on the life of the Borrower, will be effective from the date of said Note until the Note is repaid, or said group policy terminates, or the final maturity date of the Note, whichever first occurs, in an amount necessary to reduce or extinguish the Borrower's indebtedness under said Note, but not to exceed $20,000 in respect of all indebtedness of the Borrower to the Bank for which the life of the Borrower may have been insured under said group life insurance policy, the proceeds of which insurance shall be paid to the Bank for application to the discharge of such indebtedness. If an identifiable charge is to be made to the Borrower for such insurance, the amount thereof will be set forth at Item (6) of the Note on the reverse side hereof. If any such insurance for which an identifiable charge has been made to the Borrower is declined by the insurer or otherwise does not become effective, the Borrower will be given immediate notice thereof and any such charge paid by the Borrower will be promptly refunded. The Borrower will receive a certificate of insurance relative to any insurance effected on his life within 30 days of the date of the Note.

BORROWER TO SIGN IF IDENTIFIABLE CHARGE IS MADE

THE APPLICATION FOR CREDIT EVIDENCED BY THE NOTE ON THE REVERSE SIDE OF THIS FORM HAS BEEN:

☐ **WITHDRAWN** – THE ACCOMODATION REQUESTED CANNOT BE GRANTED AT THIS TIME EXCEPT ON THE TERMS OR CONDITIONS OFFERED TO YOU. THIS DECISION WAS BASED IN PART:

☐ **DECLINED** – THE DECISION NOT TO GRANT THE ACCOMODATION REQUESTED AT THIS TIME WAS BASED IN PART:

☐ ON INFORMATION, NOT NECESSARILY OF A DEROGATORY NATURE, CONTAINED IN A CONSUMER REPORT FROM THE CONSUMER REPORTING AGENCY(S) LISTED BELOW.

☐ ON INFORMATION, NOT NECESSARILY OF A DEROGATORY NATURE, OBTAINED FROM SOURCES OTHER THAN A CONSUMER REPORTING AGENCY. YOU MAY, WITHIN SIXTY DAYS OF THE RECEIPT OF THIS DISCLOSURE, SUBMIT A WRITTEN REQUEST FOR THE REASONS FOR OUR DECISION.

SIGNATURE   DATE

SUMMARY OF CERTAIN SECTIONS OF ARTICLE 3–A OF THE PERSONAL PROPERTY LAW OF THE STATE OF NEW YORK:

§ 46-c • An assignment of earnings (Assignment) shall be contained in a separate written instrument, and at its top and just above the place reserved for the signature of the assignor, must be described in at least 10 point bold type, as an assignment of wages, etc.; it must contain the name and address of the assignee and, in its text or in a writing permanently attached, identify specifically and describe fully the transaction to which it relates, the amount of the indebtedness, the dates on which and place at which payments are to be made, and that if secures only the transaction or series of transactions described in such assignment.

§ 46-e • The Assignment must be personally executed by the assignor and a copy of it, and of any papers attached thereto, together with a copy of any papers executed by the assignor pertaining to the transaction described in the Assignment, must be delivered to the assignor before the same is filed with the employer.

§ 46-f • Except as provided by Article 9 of the New York Banking Law, the charges made by the assignee must not exceed a greater sum than 18% per annum on the amount of the loan or advance, except as permitted by Section 5-531 of the General Obligations Law of New York.

§ 48 • Before an Assignment (except assignments given as security for money actually advanced to or at the request of the assignor by any bank, trust company or credit union doing business in the State of New York) shall be filed with an employer:
   (a) the assignor must be at least 21 days in default on a payment, and after such default the assignee must have mailed to the assignor by certified mail, return receipt requested, a copy of the Assignment and any attached papers with a written notice that, unless the amount in default shall be paid within 20 days from the date of the mailing, the Assignment will be served on the assignor's employer, and advising assignor of his right to a hearing on the validity of the Assignment (pursuant to S 47-e, below) and any defense to the underlying debt;
   (b) if the assignor notifies the assignee of a defense, the assignee cannot file the Assignment until it obtains a court order;
   (c) the written notice given the assignor must instruct him to bring the notice with him and have any payment endorsed thereon and, if a payment is so endorsed, or if the assignor receives, a written receipt referring to the notice, the Assignment cannot be served on the employer until subsequent default and similar notice.
   (d) if the notice is returned undelivered, it may then be served the same as a summons or mailed to the Assignee by certified mail, return receipt requested, where he works.

§ 47-e • With the exception of an order made by a family court or in a matrimonial proceeding, the assignor, his employer or any other interested party may commence a special proceeding to vacate the Assignment in the county where assignee or assignor resides or where the Assignment is filed. The court may consider any defense to the Assignment and underlying debt, with burden of proof on each to be on the Assignee, and may grant appropriate interim relief. If vacated by a judgment it may be presented to the county clerk.

§ 48-a • No amount is deductible from the assignor's future earnings until at least 10 days have elapsed after a true and authenticated copy of the Assignment together with an itemized statement of the amount then due the assignee, has been filed with the employer, and, if the assignment relates to indebtedness of less than $1,000: (a) the amount collectible in any month can be not more than 10% of the assignor's earnings in that month: (b) it is subordinate to any prior assignment, income execution or order under Section 5226 of the Civil Practice Law and Rules of New York.

§ 48-b • No amount is deductible from the assignor's future earnings unless the same exceed, $85 per week.

§ 48-c • Unemployment by the assignor at the time of or subsequent to the Assignment does not prevent the Assignment from becoming effective later.

§ 49 • Banks, Trust Companies and Credit Unions doing business in the state of New York are not required to file such an Assignment with any public office or officer.

AFTER

First National City Bank

Consumer Loan Note   Date_____, 19____

(In this note, the words **I, me, mine** and **my** mean each and all of those who signed it. The words **you, your** and **yours** mean First National City Bank.)

Terms of Repayment To repay my loan, I promise to pay you_____Dollars ($_____). I'll pay this sum at one of your branches in_____ uninterrupted_____ installments of $_____each. Payments will be due_____, starting from the date the loan is made.

Here's the breakdown of my payments:

1. Amount of the Loan $_____
2. Property Insurance Premium $_____
3. Filing Fee for
   Security Interest $_____
4. Amount Financed (1+2+3) $_____
5. **Finance Charge** $_____
6. Total of Payments (4+5) $_____

Annual Percentage Rate_____%

Prepayment of Whole Note Even though I needn't pay more than the fixed installments, I have the right to prepay the whole outstanding amount of this note at any time. If I do, or if this loan is refinanced—that is, replaced by a new note— you will refund the unearned **finance charge,** figured by the rule of 78—a commonly used formula for figuring rebates on installment loans. However, you can charge a minimum **finance charge** of $10.

Late Charge If I fall more than 10 days behind in paying an installment, I promise to pay a late charge of 5% of the overdue installment, but no more than $5. However, the sum total of late charges on all installments can't be more than 2% of the total of payments or $25, whichever is less.

Security To protect you if I default on this or any other debt to you, I give you what is known as a security interest in my ○ Motor Vehicle and/or_____ (see the Security Agreement I have given you for a full description of this property), ○ Stocks, ○ Bonds, ○ Savings Account (more fully described in the receipt you gave me today) **and** any account or other property of mine coming into your possession.

Insurance I understand I must maintain property insurance on the property covered by the Security Agreement for its full insurable value, but I can buy this insurance through a person of my own choosing.

Default I'll be in default:
1. If I don't pay an installment on time; or
2. If any other creditor tries by legal process to take any money of mine in your possession.

You can then demand immediate payment of the balance of this note, minus the part of the **finance charge** which hasn't been earned figured by the rule of 78. You will also have other legal rights, for instance, the right to repossess, sell and apply security to the payments under this note and any other debts I may then owe you.

Irregular Payments You can accept late payments or partial payments, even though marked "payment in full", without losing any of your rights under this note.

Delay in Enforcement You can delay enforcing any of your rights under this note without losing them.

Collection Costs If I'm in default under this note and you demand full payment, I agree to pay you interest on the unpaid balance at the rate of 1% per month, after an allowance for the unearned **finance charge.** If you have to sue me, I also agree to pay your attorney's fees equal to 15% of the amount due, and court costs. But if I defend and the court decides I am right, I understand that you will pay my reasonable attorney's fees and the court costs.

Comakers If I'm signing this note as a comaker, I agree to be equally responsible with the borrower. You don't have to notify me that this note hasn't been paid. You can change the terms of payment and release any security without notifying or releasing me from responsibility on this note.

Copy Received The borrower acknowledges receipt of a completely filled-in copy of this note.

Signatures   Addresses

Borrower:_____   _____

Comaker:_____   _____

Comaker:_____   _____

Comaker:_____   _____

Hot Line If something should happen and you can't pay on time, please call us immediately at (212) 559-3061.

Personal Finance Department
First National City Bank

Several years ago we were asked by IRS lawyers to rewrite a particularly technical, complex regulation governing the deductibility of bad debts. Along with polishing the language, we also made suggestions for typography and layout.[4]

These considerations are not simply mechanical; they make an important and salutary difference to the comprehensibility of the regulation. Format, order, spacing, and size of print all seriously affect the clarity of written material. Compare the language of the regulation with our recommended version.

BEFORE

§ 1.166–1 Bad debts

(a) Allowance of deduction. Section 166 provides that, in computing taxable income under section 63, a deduction shall be allowed in respect of bad debts owed to the taxpayer. For this purpose, bad debts shall, subject to the provisions of section 166 and the regulations thereunder, be taken into account either as—

(1) A deduction in respect of debts which become worthless in whole or in part; or as

(2) A deduction for a reasonable addition to a reserve for bad debts.

(b) Manner of selecting method. (1) A taxpayer filing a return of income for the first taxable year for which he is entitled to a bad debt deduction may select either of the two methods prescribed by paragraph (a) of this section for treating bad debts, but such selection is subject to the approval of the district director upon examination of the return. If the method so selected is approved, it shall be used in returns for all subsequent taxable years unless the Commissioner grants permission to use the other method. A statement of facts substantiating any deduction claimed under section 166 on account of bad debts shall accompany each return of income.

(2) Taxpayers who have properly selected one of the two methods for treating bad debts under provisions of prior law corresponding to section 166 shall continue to use that method for all subsequent taxable years unless the Commissioner grants permission to use the other method.

(3) (i) For taxable years beginning after December 31, 1959, application for permission to change the method of treating bad debts shall be made in accordance with section 446(e) and paragraph (e) (3) of § 1.446–1.

(ii) For taxable years beginning before January 1, 1960, application for permission to change the method of treating bad debts shall be made at least 30 days before the close of the taxable year for which the change is effective.

(c) Bona fide debt required. Only a bona fide debt qualifies for purposes of section 166. A bona fide debt is a debt which arises from a debtor-creditor relationship based upon a valid and enforceable obligation to pay a fixed or determinable sum of money. A gift or contribution to capital shall not be considered a debt for purposes of section 166. The fact that a bad debt is not due at the time of deduction shall not of itself prevent its allowance under section 166.

(d) Amount deductible—(1) General rule. Except in the case of a deduction for a reasonable addition to a reserve for bad debts, the basis for determining the amount of deduction under section 166 in respect of a bad debt shall be the same as the adjusted basis prescribed by § 1.1011–1 for determining the loss from the sale or other disposition of property. To determine the allowable deduction in the case of obligations acquired before March 1, 1913, see also paragraph (b) of § 1.1053–1.

(2) Specific cases. Subject to any provision of section 166 and the regulations thereunder which provides to the contrary, the following amounts are deductible as bad debts:

(i) Notes or accounts receivable. (a) If, in computing taxable income, a taxpayer values his notes or accounts receivable at their fair market value when received, the amount deductible as a bad debt under section 166 in respect of such receivables shall be limited to such fair market value even though it is less than their face value.

(b) A purchaser of accounts receivable which become worthless during the taxable year shall be entitled under section 166 to a deduction which is based upon the price he paid for such receivables but not upon their face value.

(ii) Bankruptcy claim. Only the difference between the amount received in distribution of the assets of a bankrupt and the amount of the claim may be deducted under section 166 as a bad debt.

(iii) Claim against decedent's estate. The excess of the amount of the claim over the amount received by a creditor of a decedent in distribution of the assets of the decedent's estate may be considered a worthless debt under section 166.

(c) Prior inclusion in income required. Worthless debts arising from unpaid wages, salaries, fees, rents, and similar items of taxable income shall not be allowed as a deduction under section 166 unless the income such items represent has been included in the return of income for the year for which the deduction as a bad debt is claimed or for a prior taxable year.

(f) Recovery of bad debts. Any amount attributable to the recovery during the taxable year of a bad debt, or of a part of a bad debt, which was allowed as a deduction from gross income in a prior taxable year shall be included in gross income for the taxable year of recovery, except to the extent that the recovery is excluded from gross income under the provisions of § 1.111–1, relating to the recovery of certain items previously deducted or credited. This paragraph shall not apply, however, to a bad debt which was previously charged against a reserve by a taxpayer on the reserve method of treating bad debts.

(g) Worthless securities. (1) Section 166 and the regulations thereunder do not apply to a debt which is evidenced by a bond, debenture, note, or certificate, or other evidence of indebtedness, issued by a corporation or by a government or political subdivision thereof, with interest coupons or in registered form. See section 166(c). For provisions allowing the deduction of a loss resulting from the worthlessness of such a debt, see § 1.165–5.

(2) The provisions of subparagraph (1) of this paragraph do not apply to any loss sustained by a bank and resulting from the worthlessness of a security described in section 165(g) (2) (C). See paragraph (a) of § 1.582–1. As added T.D. 6403, July 31, 1959, 24 F.R. 6160.

AFTER

a. *Allowance of deduction for bad debts*
   A taxpayer who is unable to collect a fixed sum of money agreed upon in a valid agreement with a corporation or another person, even with a relative, has a "bad debt." This term does not apply to such things as gifts, contributions, or other losses.

   Under Section 166, taxpayers are allowed to deduct bad debts when they compute their taxable income according to the instructions in Section 63. They may take these bad debts into account in either of two ways:
   (1) As a bad debt that has become wholly or partly worthless;
   (2) As a bad business debt that requires reasonable addition to a fund to cover bad debts. The reserve for bad debts is described in §1.166–4 of these Regulations.

b. *What qualifies as a deductible bad debt*
   Only an actual bad debt qualifies under Section 166. That is, debts can be deducted only if they result from a taxpayer's being unable to collect a fixed sum of money agreed upon in a valid agreement with another person or business entity. Gifts, contributions to businesses, or payments into funds used to provide capital to found or operate a business may not be deducted. Even if a bad

debt is not due at the time of deduction, it may still be allowed under Section 166. It is deductible if it had value at the beginning of the year but no value at the end of the year. In other words, a bad debt is deductible when it becomes wholly worthless, or in the case of a business debt, is deductible when it becomes partially worthless. Worthlessness is more fully described in Section 1.166–2 and Section 1.166–3 of these Regulations.

c. *Choosing a method for deducting bad debts*
Before taxpayers can deduct bad debts, they must choose one of the two methods described in paragraph (a). This choice is subject to the approval of an IRS District Director when the taxpayer's return is examined. If the District Director has approved the choice, taxpayers should continue to treat the bad debt in the same manner in all later tax returns. They should also file a statement of facts to support the claim of deduction with every tax return filed in later years. If for some reason taxpayers later want to change their methods for treating a bad debt, they must first have the change approved by the IRS Commissioner. Also, taxpayers who are already treating bad debts under the provisions of an earlier law should continue to treat them in the same way unless the IRS Commissioner approves a change to one of the two methods described in paragraph (a).

d. *How and when to apply for a change of methods*
This depends on what taxable year is involved.
  (i) *After December 31, 1959.* To change the method for treating a bad debt for taxable years *after* December 31, 1959, the taxpayers must first get permission from the IRS Commissioner. To do this, they should follow the instructions in Section 446(e) of the Internal Revenue Code and paragraph (e)(3) of Section 1.446–1 of these Regulations, filing the request within 180 days after the beginning of the taxable year for which the change is to be effective.
  (ii) *Before January 1, 1960.* To change the method for treating a bad debt for taxable years *before* January 1, 1960, taxpayers must first get permission from the IRS Commissioner. To do this they should apply for the change not less than 30 days before the close of the taxable year for which the change is to be effective.

e. *How much is deductible*
General Rule: Under Section 166 of the Internal Revenue Code, the method for determining how much to deduct for a bad debt is the same as the method for determining the loss from the sale of property described in Section 1.1011–1 of these Regulations. The

exception to that general rule is if the deduction is for a reasonable addition to a reserve for bad debts, which is only permitted for business debts.

If taxpayers are claiming deductions for bad debts acquired before March 1, 1913, they should also see paragraph (c) or Section 1.1053–1 of these Regulations.

f. *Specific cases*

Depending on the type, different amounts of bad debts are deductible. Unless some other provision of Section 166 of the Code or these Regulations prevents it, the following amounts are deductible as bad debts:

(1) *Notes or Accounts Receivable.* A taxpayer may deduct the fair market value of a note or account receivable if the taxpayer, when determining his taxable income, bases his income on the fair market value of the note or account receivable. The taxpayer who determines taxable income by using the fair market value of the note or receivable may not deduct the face value of the note, even if it is higher than the fair market value. Similarly, a taxpayer who buys accounts receivable is entitled to a deduction based on the price paid, not the face value of the account.

(2) *Bankruptcy.* A taxpayer may deduct only the difference between the amount claimed from the bankrupt and the amount the taxpayer received.

(3) *Decedent's Estates.* A taxpayer may deduct only the difference between the amount claimed from the estate and the amount the taxpayer received.

g. *Reported income*

Certain bad debts are not deductible unless the sum in question is reported or was reported as income. Examples include bad debts from unpaid wages, salaries, fees, and rents.

h. *Bad debts that are later paid*

A taxpayer must report as income any amount received that has been deducted as a bad debt. This rule does not apply to business debts that were charged against a reserve for such debts, nor does it apply to debts received under Section 1.111–1 of these Regulations.

i. *Securities*

Section 1.165–5 of these Regulations discusses when a taxpayer may deduct a debt which is based on the indebtedness of a corporation or a government entity. This kind of indebtedness is frequently represented by a bond, debenture, note, or certificate. Subsections a through g above are not applicable to the indebtedness of a corporation or government entity, nor are they applicable to a bank that suffers a bad debt based on the worthlessness of a security as described in Section 1.582 of these Regulations.

Legislative draftsmanship has special requirements, and to some extent the amount of editing that can be made by a plain-English law advocate is limited. Nevertheless, both the language and the format of most legislation could be shortened, clarified, and improved dramatically. Since over 45,000 laws are passed by federal and state legislatures annually,[5] the impact of improvements could be vast.

As an example of what might be done, consider a relatively finite and simple bill that was introduced in the Maryland House of Delegates a few years ago. The two-page bill—reprinted verbatim below—had to do with the state's requirements pertaining to out-of-state alcoholic beverage dealers. We asked a bright young attorney what it meant and if she could improve the writing. After four hours, she presented us with the after version presented below. The nature of the text does not permit legislation like this to be transformed into Cole Porter lyrics, but the traditional hieroglyphics of most legislation could be radically reformed despite its technical and prosaic content. If busy legislators or their legal staffs do not have time to edit proposed laws, a great public service would be performed if they hired a stylist to do the task.

BEFORE

HOUSE OF DELEGATES

91r0793   No. 92   0100–02200
                        (PRE-FILED)

By: Delegate Exum
Requested: November 27, 1978
Introduced and read first time: January 1, 1979
Assigned to: Economic Matters
Committee report: Favorable with amendments
House action: Adopted with floor amendments
Read second time: February 28, 1979
                    CHAPTER _____
AN ACT concerning
        Alcoholic Beverages—Nonresident Dealer Permit
FOR the purpose of specifying to whom nonresident alcoholic beverage

dealer permits may be issued; permitting certain actions concerning certain goods by the holders of these permits; and generally relating to nonresident alcoholic beverage dealers.

BY repealing and reenacting, with amendments,

Article 2B—Alcoholic Beverages

Section 4(h)

Annotated Code of Maryland

(1976 Replacement Volume and 1978 Supplement)

SECTION 1. BE IT ENACTED BY THE GENERAL ASSEMBLY OF MARYLAND, That section(s) of the Annotated Code of Maryland be repealed, amended, or enacted to read as follows:

Article 2B—Alcoholic Beverages

4.

(h) [Such a permit shall authorize the holder thereof to sell, consign, and deliver alcoholic beverages from a location outside Maryland to persons in Maryland who are authorized to receive same under this article. Provided, however, no such permit shall be required to make direct sales and shipments into this State from a location outside the continental limits and possessions of the United States.]

(1) A NONRESIDENT DEALER'S PERMIT, FOR THE PURPOSE OF SELLING BEER, WINE, OR DISTILLED SPIRITS TO MARYLAND LICENSEES AUTHORIZED TO RECEIVE THOSE BEVERAGES, MAY BE ISSUED ONLY TO:

(I) A BREWER, DISTILLER, RECTIFIER, BOTTLER, MANUFACTURER, VINTNER, OR WINERY; OR

(II) A SALES AGENT OF ONE OF THOSE UNDER SUBPARAGRAPH (I) OF THIS PARAGRAPH, PROVIDED PROOF OF THAT AGENCY IS PRESENTED THAT IS SATISFACTORY TO THE COMPTROLLER; OR

(III) AN IMPORTER OF BEER, WINE, OR DISTILLED BEVERAGES PRODUCED OUTSIDE THE UNITED STATES; OR

(IV) AN AMERICAN SALES AGENT OF AN IMPORTER UNDER SUBPARAGRAPH (III) OF THIS PARAGRAPH, PROVIDED PROOF OF THAT AGENCY IS PRESENTED THAT IS SATISFACTORY TO THE COMPTROLLER.

(2) A HOLDER OF A NONRESIDENT DEALER'S PERMIT MAY SELL, CONSIGN, OR DELIVER, FROM A LOCATION OUTSIDE MARYLAND, TO PERSONS IN MARYLAND WHO ARE AUTHORIZED TO RECEIVE THEM, ONLY THOSE BEERS, WINES, OR DISTILLED SPIRITS WHICH IT DISTILLS, RECTIFIES, BOTTLES, MANUFACTURES, OR REPRESENTS AS THE DESIGNATED SALES AGENT. THE BREWER, DISTILLER, RECTIFIER, BOTTLER, MANUFACTURER, VINTNER, WINERY, IMPORTER AND THEIR DESIGNATED AGENT MAY NOT DISCRIMINATE DIRECTLY OR INDIRECTLY IN PRICE BETWEEN MARYLAND LICENSEES.

(3) NOTWITHSTANDING ANY OTHER PROVISION OF THIS SECTION, ANY BRAND OF BEER PRESENTLY BEING SOLD, CONSIGNED, OR DELIVERED IN MARYLAND BY THE HOLDER OF A NONRESIDENT DEALER'S PERMIT FROM A LOCA-

TION OUTSIDE MARYLAND TO PERSONS IN MARYLAND WHO ARE AUTHORIZED TO RECEIVE IT UNDER THIS ARTICLE MAY CONTINUE TO BE SOLD, CONSIGNED, OR DELIVERED UNTIL SUCH TIME AS THE BREWER, THE IMPORTER, OR DESIGNATED SALES AGENT OF THE BREWER OR THE IMPORTER OF THAT BRAND OF BEER PREEMPTS THE SALES TERRITORY BY APPOINTING A FRAN-CHISEE AS PROVIDED IN SECTIONS 203A THROUGH 203G, INCLUSIVE, OF THIS ARTICLE.

(4) NOTWITHSTANDING ANY OTHER PROVISION OF THIS SECTION, A NON-RESIDENT DEALER'S PERMIT IS NOT REQUIRED TO MAKE DIRECT SALES AND SHIPMENTS INTO THIS STATE FROM A LOCATION OUTSIDE THE CONTINENTAL LIMITS AND POSSESSIONS OF THE UNITED STATES.

SECTION 2. AND BE IT FURTHER ENACTED, That this Act shall take effect July 1, 1979.

EXPLANATION: SMALL CAPITALS INDICATE MATTER ADDED TO EXISTING LAW.
[Brackets] indicate matter deleted from existing law.
Underlining indicates amendments to bill.

AFTER

HOUSE OF DELEGATES

9110793   No. 92   0100–02200
(PRE-FILED)
The headings, being required style, are repeated.
CHAPTER _____

Subject: Alcoholic Beverage Dealer Permits for Nonresidents

Purpose:

(1) to specify the persons or entities eligible for alcoholic beverage dealer permits for nonresidents; and

(2) to specify restrictions on the actions of holders of these permits.

Effect: This Act repeals and reenacts, with amendments

Article 2B—Alcoholic Beverages

Section 4(h)

Annotated Code of Maryland

(1976 Replacement Volume and 1978 Supplement)

The Act:

SECTION 1. Effective July 1, 1979, the following changes and additions in Article 2B, Section 4(h) of the Annotated Code of Maryland regarding alcoholic beverages are hereby enacted by the General Assembly of Maryland:

The following paragraph from Section 4(h) is deleted:

Such a permit shall authorize the holder thereof to sell, consign, and deliver alcoholic beverages from a location outside Maryland to persons in Maryland who are authorized to receive same under this article. Provided, however, no such permit shall be required to make direct sales and shipments into this State from a location outside the continental limits and possessions of the United States. The following paragraphs have been added to the existing law:

1. ELIGIBILITY REQUIREMENTS

(I) PERMITS MAY ONLY BE ISSUED TO THE FOLLOWING NONRESIDENTS OF MARYLAND WHO WISH TO SELL, CONSIGN, OR DELIVER ALCOHOLIC BEVERAGES TO THOSE IN MARYLAND AUTHORIZED TO RECEIVE THEM ("LICENSEES"): A. BREWERS, B. DISTILLERS, C. RECTIFIERS, D. BOTTLERS, E. VINTNERS, F. WINERIES, G. IMPORTERS OF ALCOHOLIC BEVERAGES PRODUCED OUTSIDE THE UNITED STATES, H. AMERICAN SALES AGENTS FOR ANY OF THE ABOVE, PROVIDED THAT THE COMPTROLLER IS PRESENTED SATISFACTORY PROOF OF THE AGENCY.

2. RESTRICTIONS ON PERMIT HOLDERS

(I) DEALERS WITH NONRESIDENT PERMITS ("PERMIT HOLDERS") MAY ONLY SELL, CONSIGN, OR DELIVER ALCOHOLIC BEVERAGES FROM OUTSIDE MARYLAND TO MARYLAND LICENSEES.

(II) THE ALCOHOLIC BEVERAGES REFERRED TO IN 2(I) ABOVE ARE LIMITED TO ONLY THOSE WHICH THE PERMIT HOLDER DISTILLS, RECTIFIES, BOTTLES, MANUFACTURES, PRODUCES, IMPORTS, OR REPRESENTS AS A SALES AGENT.

(III) A PERMIT HOLDER MAY NOT INTENTIONALLY CHARGE VARYING PRICES AMONG MARYLAND LICENSEES NOR USE ANY PRICING PRACTICE WHICH HAS THE EFFECT OF DOING SO.

(IV) A BREWER OR IMPORTER OF BEER MAY PREEMPT A PERMIT SALES HOLDER'S TERRITORY BY APPOINTING A FRANCHISE PURSUANT TO SECTIONS 203A–203G OF THIS ARTICLE.

3. DIRECT SALES FROM OUTSIDE THE UNITED STATES

(I) DEALER MAKING DIRECT SALES AND SHIPMENTS INTO MARYLAND FROM OUTSIDE THE UNITED STATES AND ITS POSSESSIONS DO NOT REQUIRE THIS PERMIT.

EXPLANATION: SMALL CAPITALS INDICATE MATTER ADDED TO EXISTING LAW.
  Text without capitals indicates the existing law.
  Underlining indicates amendments to bill.

Jury instructions could also stand improvement. The public decides most serious criminal cases and civil disputes through juries instructed in what amounts to a foreign language.

A very wise but folksy judge in the Federal Court in Kentucky began his jury instructions by telling the jurors an anecdote. "When Andrew Johnson was a federal judge in Tennessee," he remarked as he swiveled his chair around to face the jurors, "he used to tell the jurors who heard his cases, 'You've heard the evidence; now go out and do right by these people.' " He wished he could do the same, but he was required to do more. He then expounded the set jury instructions approved and used by federal judges.

This judge did a good job translating the complex rules that jurors are supposed to apply in deciding the facts of the cases they hear. But we wonder whether the sophisticated charges are as good as the simple admonition of Andrew Johnson.

Our experiences suggest that jurors are often confused and misled by the instructions proposed to them by judges. Recent studies[6] have confirmed that our impressions are correct.

The National Science Foundation, the National Institute of Mental Health, and the Justice Department's Law Enforcement Assistance Administration have all sponsored studies of jury instructions. An actual criminal trial for attempted murder and a mock Florida burglary case were videotaped and were shown to selected (and paid) panels of jurors. The aim was to determine whether standard jury instructions could be improved and made more comprehensible. Different results flowed from the instructions before and after they were rewritten; not unxpectedly, the edited versions led to more correct and stable decision-making by jurors, often in crucial respects. As a result, the analysts concluded, fairer trials with more just (correct) results could be expected from more comprehensible jury instructions.

Comparable studies[7] of mock civil jury trials have been reported, showing that crucial mistakes were made by jurors because of their misconceptions about the meaning of common instructions such as the one governing contributory negligence.

The jury system is an imperfect one, and it can never be corrected to administer perfectly just decisions. Indeed, some of its vagaries were designed for good reasons, such as the inherent right of juries to ignore the law and decide cases on emotional grounds. Nonetheless, the jury system's acceptable and inevitable imperfection must be contained; unnecessary, unproductive defects should be avoided. Technical and ritualistic instructions sound like a foreign language to most jurors.

This problem could be corrected to a great degree if experts were to analyze and redraft problematic instructions; if jurors were instructed before and after trials; and if judges were to give written instructions. Since in almost all courts jury instructions have been standardized for the last half century[8] (before 1930, the lawyers in each case worked out their own set with the trial judge), it would be feasible to establish a set of nationally sanctioned instructions tailored, where necessary, to local needs and expressed in plain English. Consider the difference between the following two sets of instructions:

Reasonable Doubt

BEFORE

A reasonable doubt is one based on reason. It is not mere possible doubt, but is such a doubt as would govern or control a person in the more weighty affairs of life. If the minds of the jurors, after the entire comparison and consideration of all the evidence, are in such a condition that they can say they feel an abiding conviction of the truth of the charge, there is not a reasonable doubt. Doubt to be reasonable must be actual and substantial, not mere possibility or speculation.

AFTER

A REASONABLE DOUBT is the kind of doubt that would stop a person with common sense from making an extremely important decision in his/her own life. Notice that when I say that you should be so convinced that you do not have a reasonable doubt about it, I am not saying that you have to be 100 percent convinced. Use your common sense about this. Nothing in life is absolutely certain, but this does not stop us from making decisions in our own lives. Thus, all that we can ask of you is to be as certain as you would want to be if you were making an important decision in your own life.

Malice Aforethought

Malice aforethought, as used in the definition of Attempted Murder, means the intentional doing of a wrongful act without legal cause of excuse or what the law considers adequate provocation. The condition of mind described as malice aforethought may arise, not alone from anger, hatred, revenge, or from particular ill will, spite, or grudge toward the person

WHAT CAN CAUSE SOMEONE TO HAVE AN EVIL WISH TO HURT?
An evil wish to hurt someone can be caused in two ways:
1. By recklessness and neglect toward others in general.
2. By bad feelings toward someone in particular.
Some of you may think that recklessness toward other people in

wounded, but may result from any unjustifiable or unlawful motive or purpose to injure another, which proceeds from a heart fatally bent on mischief or with reckless disregard of consequences and social duty. Malice aforethought does not imply deliberation or the lapse of any considerable time between the malicious intention, but denotes rather an unlawful purpose and design in contradistinction to accident and mischance.

general is worse than bad feelings toward someone in particular. Thus, you may feel that an evil wish to hurt caused by the first reason is worse than that caused by the second reason. This is not true under the law.

According to our laws, it does not matter what caused a person's evil wish to hurt someone. A person is just as guilty when his/her evil wish to hurt is caused by bad feelings toward someone in particular as when it is caused by a neglect for people in general.

An earlier study by a law professor and a linguistic expert, funded by the National Science Foundation, had concluded that "jury instructions are inadequately understood," but that well-accepted methods were available to improve the comprehensibility of this special form of legal language.[9]

These researchers tested a group of people who had been called to jury duty in Prince George's County, Maryland, to assess their understanding and application of fourteen standard California civil jury instructions in a traffic accident case. When they cleaned up the language, eliminating excess verbiage and unnecessary passive constructions, they found that the test group's understanding improved. By eliminating multiple negatives, properly placing phrases, and organizing paragraphs better, the researchers were able to improve the jurors' performance significantly. Here are two examples—a straightforward instruction about process and a complex one about the law of a case—before and after the changes were made:

The Meaning of the Judge's Instructions

BEFORE

If in these instructions any rule, direction or idea is repeated or stated in varying ways, no emphasis thereon is intended by me and

AFTER

As you listen to these instructions of law, there are three things to keep in mind:

First, throughout these instruc-

none must be inferred by you. For that reason you are not to single out any certain sentence or any individual point or instruction and ignore the others, but you are to consider all the instructions as a whole and are to regard each in the light of all the others.

The order in which the instructions are given has no significance as to their relative importance.

tions, you may find that some ideas or rules of law are repeated. That does not mean that I am trying to emphasize those rules or ideas.

Second, you must consider all the instructions together, as a package, and you must not ignore any instruction or any party of an instruction.

Third, the fact that I am giving the instructions in a particular order does not mean that the first are more important than the last, or vice-versa. In other words, the order has no significance.

Assumption of Risk

BEFORE

If plaintiff assumed the risk of harm he may not recover damages for an injury resulting therefrom.

In order for plaintiff to have assumed such risk, he must have had actual knowledge of the particular danger and an appreciation of the risk involved and the magnitude thereof, and must thereafter have voluntarily assumed such risk.

For a person to act voluntarily he must have freedom of choice. This freedom of choice must come from circumstances that provide him a reasonable opportunity, without violating any legal or moral duty, to safely refuse to expose himself to the danger in question.

In determining whether the plaintiff assumed such risk, you may consider his maturity, intel-

AFTER

If the plaintiff voluntarily took a risk and was injured as a result of taking the risk, then he cannot recover money for his injury.

In order for someone to voluntarily take a risk, he must know and understand the dangers involved, and decide to take the chance anyway.

In deciding whether the plaintiff voluntarily took a risk, you may consider his maturity and intelligence, and all the other circumstances of the case.

ligence, experience and capacity, along with all the other surrounding circumstances as shown by the evidence.

Here is a more formal variety of legal writing—an order presented to a court by a party proposing a disposition of one aspect of a case —that we took from the records of the District of Columbia Superior Court, and edited.

<table>
<tr><td align="center">BEFORE</td><td align="center">AFTER</td></tr>
<tr><td align="center">ORDER</td><td align="center">ORDER</td></tr>
</table>

BEFORE

ORDER

Upon consideration of the Plaintiff's Motion to Compel Answers to Interrogatories, and the Opposition thereto, the Record herein and the argument of Counsel in open Court, it appearing the Plaintiff served upon the Defendant a set of Interrogatories, and it further appearing that the Defendants objected to certain Interrogatories on the ground of relevance, and it further appearing that the Answers sought to be evoked by the objectionable Interrogatories are irrelevant to the instant proceedings and are not reasonably calculated to lead to further discoverable materials, and it further appearing to the Court that the Defendants' objections on the ground of relevancy are proper, it is, therefore, this _____ day of _____, 1980,

ORDERED, that the Plaintiff's Motion to Compel Answers to Interrogatories, be and the same hereby is, denied, and it is further

ORDERED, that the Plaintiff shall pay to the Defendant the

AFTER

ORDER

I have considered the Plaintiff's Motion and the Opposition, the Record and the lawyer's arguments. The Plaintiff served upon the Defendant a set of Interrogatories. The Defendants objected to certain Interrogatories on the ground of relevance. The Answers sought to be evoked by the objectionable Interrogatories are irrelevant to these proceedings and are not reasonably calculated to lead to further discoverable materials. The Defendants' objections on the ground of relevancy are proper.

Therefore, the Plaintiff's Motion to Compel Answers to Interrogatories is denied.

The Plaintiff shall pay to the Defendant the sum of $_____ representing reasonable attorney fees incurred by the Defendants to oppose the Motion.

_____

JUDGE

sum of $_____ representing reasonable attorney's fees incurred by the Defendants to oppose the Motion.

JUDGE

From the same court, here is a complaint in a civil case that brimmed with human drama until the lawyers began to narrate the story:

4. From September 1979 to the present, Defendant has intentionally caused emotional distress to Plaintiff by falsely telling her between September 1979 and August 1980 of his affection and admiration for her and insinuating himself into her affections, obtaining money from her, and cultivating her trust in him without intending to demonstrate genuine fidelity to her in return, but rather intending to obtain whatever money and other material or intangible benefits he could obtain from her no matter what false representations might be necessary for him to make to her to effect the same, and then to cast her aside without mercy and without repaying money lent by her to him or mitigating in any way the shock of her discovery of his duplicity. Defendant thus perpetrated an extreme outrage on Plaintiff's most sensitive affections, knowing her special susceptibility to his blandishments flowing from the affection for him which he caused her to feel.

Wouldn't you want to know what happened? We don't because the lawyers "perpetrated an extreme outrage" on the language.

The examples we have used are illustrative of the point we wish to make. Ordinary legal writing can be cleaner, more succinct, and more accurate. There is no need to follow traditional models; on the contrary, they can and should be avoided.

The aesthetics of good legal writing, the need to avoid legal mistakes, diminishing library space, and the rising costs of legal literature all combine to make the case for "after" writing.

7

The Ten Commandments of Legal Writing

After a long sermon on any subject, there is both an inclination and an obligation to sum up. Here, then, are ten rules that cover most of the elemental requirements for good writing.

I. WRITE LIKE A HUMAN BEING

Lawyers are ordinary people, when they are not acting like lawyers. These ordinary people, who communicate quite effectively in the course of everyday affairs, shift gears intellectually whenever they decide they should be acting like lawyers. The same lawyers who write clear and interesting letters to a kid in camp or a mother in the hospital go through a Jekyll-and-Hyde mental transformation when they sit down to write (or dictate) a business letter, a law review article, a judicial opinion, a law, a regulation, a contract, whatever. They begin writing the way they think lawyers are supposed to write. The result is stark and ludicrous.

We showed in Chapter 1 how indoctrination into legalese starts in law school, continues through lawyers' practice, and determines the language of the legislators' bills, the administrators' regulations, and the judges' opinions. As a result, the lawyers' linguistic atmosphere is polluted.

We asked a Minnesota judge why the opening paragraph of one of his opinions ran 63 words instead of the needed 32, and why the concluding paragraph ran 44 words instead of the 18 of our edited version.

He had no reason. When he became a judge, he told us, he looked at the way his predecessors and colleagues wrote their opinions and adopted their style. He was embarrassed by how his prose sounded when we read it to him aloud. He agreed shorter was better. The edited version sounded more like the man we knew. He had been acting out a role by using the ludicrous language other bad actors had traditionally used.

Just how preposterous stilted judicial writing can get is exemplified by the following excerpt from a reported decision by a Tennessee Supreme Court justice. The case concerned a woman who was injured when she fell off a toilet seat while reaching for a light cord in the dark rest room a store provided for its customers. The judge ruled that she should have known better, was contributorily negligent, and could not collect. Here is an excerpt from his reported opinion.

> When plaintiff entered this private of all places, referred to in the pleadings as a rest room, a water closet, bathroom—and by the country term privy—she looked about and saw the commode or toilet (she apparently could see the seat and seat cover thereon) and desiring more illumination in said rest room, she saw an electric light cord hanging from the ceiling, and she lowered the seat and lid, and then proceeded to mount the same on foot. This, she either accomplished or was in the act of accomplishing when she slipped or was caused to fall therefrom, landing with one foot in the commode or water closet, the other foot and rest of her body falling backward onto the floor, said fall from her perch on the closet lid causing her serious injuries.

The judge went on to ponder some of the legal doctrines governing that case, and to take judicial notice of the nature and customary use of toilets. The judge refused, however, to draw any conclusions about the ablutionary practices of what he and the defendant's lawyer referred to as members of "the feminine gender."

> The defendants, in their brief, also ask this Court to be violently presumptuous and to take judicial knowledge of the following and we quote: "that when the commode seat is in use by a member of the feminine gender that the standard or usual method of approach to it is to draw near, to then turn to face away from it, and to assume a

sitting position with a portion of the user's weight on the user's feet." This, we cannot do, for never having witnessed such a described approach, whether proper or improper, and having no desire to do so, we would have to use our jaded imagination in this respect. We have no desire to do that. So, the matter of the proper way for a person of the female gender to approach a toilet or commode is left to the conclusion of the pleader.[1]

This Tennessee judge may well have succumbed to the humor implicit in the events he was describing and was being facetious, unlike the Minnesota judge who admitted he was following the style of his brethren in a serious attempt to write like a judge. The fact is that all judges follow one another's forms and styles of writing. Their obeisance results in incantations, unnatural language, and overwriting, as a rule. No doubt the historic resort to adopting legalese as a second language led to Lord Balfour's quip: "I am talking English, not law."

This overreaching for style is not confined to judges or to formal legal documents. It is evident in the most informal writings— letters, for example. A perfectly clear-thinking, bright, and competent lawyer corresponded with one of us recently. He wished to settle a dispute between his client, an agent, and our client, a writer, over an option and an agency clause in a book contract. He introduced the terms of the agreement with this lawyerly preamble:

> In regards to the referenced matter, it is the opinion of this office that [agent's name], the literary agent concerning the aforementioned contract has an interest in the second book submitted by [author's name] to [publisher], should [publisher] accept said second book. Further, we have been noticed that the author has submitted a second book, and [publisher] has accepted said book. . . .

All this lawyer was noting was that in this case he thought his client, a book agent, had an interest in the second book our client, an author, submitted to publisher X, if the publisher accepted the book, as he knew was the case. He said as much to us when we discussed the subject. Why didn't he write the letter without all the said referenced aforementioned frills?

A South Carolina bureaucrat who attended our course showed us a letter he had written to a state legislator. He opened his letter with this sentence: "Per your request in the letter of May 16, 1979, reference Section 24 of the State Appropriations Bill, the following response is respectfully submitted." The author is a straight-talking, no-nonsense man who sounded like he was reading from a script in a strange language when we asked him to read this letter aloud. He sounded strange even to himself. He had been writing the way he thought he was supposed to write.

An official from a state insurance department, responding to an offer from our company to teach writing to insurance officials in that state, wrote us these revealing words: "Thank you for your letter of February 15, 1981, but as far as being of assistance that we feel just informing the domestic companies of the availability of your services would be sufficient."

In his famous role as Captain Spaulding in the play *Animal Crackers*, Groucho Marx parodied legal letter writing:

Honorable Charles D. Hungerdunger
c/o Hungerdunger, Hungerdunger
   & McCormick

Gentlemen?

In re yours of the 5th inst. yours to hand and in reply, I wish to state that the judiciary expenditures of this year, i.e., has not exceeded the fiscal year—brackets—this procedure is problematic and with nullification will give us a subsidiary indictment and priority. Quotes unquotes and quotes. Hoping this finds you, I beg to remain as of June 9th, Cordially, Respectfully, Regards[2]

Our friend George Rose Smith, an Arkansas Supreme Court Justice and a perceptive critic of legal writing, pointed out to a group of judges we trained that none of them would shout to their spouses: "Dear, I can't find my car keys; have you seen said keys?"; nor would they refer to their employee as "my secretary, hereinafter referred to as Cuddles . . ." If you never use the language anyplace else, why use it when you are writing as a lawyer? "What really counts in writing is exactly the same thing that counts in talking— the ability to express yourself as clearly, directly, and gracefully as possible," said Donna Woolfolk Cross in her rollicking and perceptive book, *Word Abuse*.[3]

It is a rare client or colleague or critic who will challenge this habit. One brilliant judge said to us plaintively after one of our training sessions: "For thirty years I practiced law with great success. No one—no clerk, associate, secretary, or colleague—ever criticized my writing. Now I am a judge, and again no one around me dares say anything critical about the writing in my opinions. Why hasn't someone ever told me what you fellows have just said?"

Write like a human being.

II. Think of Your Audience

Some lawyers write everything the same way, boring themselves as well as their readers. Obviously, lawyers should not strain to make artificial differences in each document. But beware of the canned form document. Without some tailoring, it may not fit.

Think about your audience before you write. Is formal or informal writing appropriate in this situation? Will it be read by one person or by the public? Will it be controversial? Is it likely to be quoted elsewhere? Are there special reasons why it should be short and general, or very detailed and thorough?

Obviously, a letter to the chief judge of your court system about a public question in which you have a mutual interest will be different from a letter to the lawyer for your client's antagonist; and both will differ from a letter you may be writing the same day to patch up a quarrel or to assist in contract negotiations. Even letters to the same audience on different occasions should be written differently. A letter to the local judge written on behalf of your client will differ from the earlier letter, and both of them will differ from the one you write to that judge inviting him to a bar-association or law-school-alumni affair.

The question of audience is especially difficult for judges, who must address many audiences at once. Are they writing solely for the parties in the particular case? Are they writing for posterity on an important and precedential subject? Will the press report this opinion? Should they write with an eye to the next appellate court's perspective? And of course, should the opinion be written at all? The answers to these questions should determine the nature and the style of the judge's opinion in that case. Each opinion should be different because the answers to these questions will vary from case to case.

The practicing lawyer should remember and apply this rule, too. Because they are busy, lawyers too often fail to write anything.

They dictate. Dictating is a good way to get a first draft, but it is no way to write a polished final project.

Busy lawyers also commonly use standard forms for common documents—wills, deeds, mortgages, divorce petitions, and so forth. Forms are acceptable if they were well-written in the first place, and if they are carefully cut each time to fit the individual client.

In their more formal writings, everything except memos and letters, lawyers often use forms and old boilerplate. Partly, they say, because they are too busy to write new forms for each instance of a recurring situation. Partly, we suspect, because they feel safe reciting the established ritual, the incantations that have, as they remind us, been given precise meaning by centuries of usage. But sometimes the ritual misfires. A New York court once decided that a canned clause a lawyer had stuck in a will instructing that "the executor pay all my just debts" revived a debt that had been barred by the statute of limitations. The testator no doubt turned over in his grave, and the legitimate heirs wished the witless attorney a speedy trip to his.

We remember seeing this touching legend on the garbage cans in the streets of Edinburgh: "The amenity of our streets is commended to your care." It was so much more refined than the signs we saw in the New York City subways: "Don't spit." Both statements were suited to their time and place; thus both were appropriate to their audience. Therefore, both worked.

III. Do Not Use Jargon (Unless You Have To)

Every group has its own special language. Teenagers, astronauts, sociologists, and doctors all communicate with each other effectively, despite their use of language few others understand. The special language of lawyers, however, can be troublesome, because lawyers have to communicate not only with each other but also with the public, in cases where the stakes can be very high! Clubby inside lingo is acceptable if it is confined to members of the club talking or writing informally to each other. And it is acceptable to express concepts that cannot be expressed economically in ordinary English. It is impermissible when lawyers are dealing for and with others, and when they retreat into their obscure language to say what could be said plainly.

The two chief examples of jargon are foreign language and arcane words.

a. *Foreign language is for foreigners.* Lawyers love foreign words and phrases. They know their audiences usually are unfamiliar with these words, but the words sound so good, so erudite, that lawyers cannot resist tossing them into their writing.

Some foreign words have become so common through usage that they are part of everybody's everyday lexicon, words such as *déjà vu*, *vice versa* and *prima facie*, and no one objects to them. But few people would say *corpus delecti* when they mean the dead body, or *nunc pro tunc* when they mean retroactively, or *seriatim* when they mean consecutively. By the time most law students get out of law school, they write and sound like they were educated at the Vatican.

The source of this linguistic habit was explored by one law professor[4] who explained that American legal language grew out of Old English common law, enriched by the Latinate traditions of the early Church and the tradition of civil law brought to England, along with the Norman French, during the Conquest. As a result, Anglo-American law is still flecked with French phrases such as *cy pres* and *fee tail*, old English words such as *deed* and *manslaughter*, Latinisms such as *subpoena* and *res ipsa loquitur*, and combinations such as *will* (Old English) and *testament* (Latin).

All law students learn these words and phrases when they thumb through legal dictionaries and hornbooks, and read venerable court decisions. It is appropriate to teach the law of trespass by explaining the historic differences between trespass *quare clausum fregit* and trespass *de bonis asportatis*. It helps the learning process. However, the practitioner should not toss those phrases at a client when explaining the basis of a case dealing with one farmer's having cut down another's trees. When my dentist or doctor starts explaining the cause of my toothache or headache in fancy and incomprehensible medical lingo, I stop him and ask him to talk to me so I can understand him. Clients should say the same thing to their lawyers when they start that act.

b. *The 50¢ word.* Akin to the habit of using foreign language to impress clients and colleagues is the equally phony practice of using the 50¢ English word when the everyday 10¢ model would do. Here again lawyers must plead guilty to killing the English language by suffocating it with notwithstandings and heretofores and whereases.

Highfalutin words produce an affectatious overloaded, pseudo-intellectual parlance that would be laughable as a parody on the stage. Lawyers do not talk about their cases; they talk about their matters: "I had an interesting matter the other day." There is nothing awkward about the word *matter*, as in "what is the matter"; it is phony when the Latin phrase *in re* is translated and used without adaptation.

A single case involving John's giving Jane money to perform some simple service usually gets translated into the party of the first part providing the party of the second part with consideration, if it doesn't go so far as to become a quid pro quo between the promisor and the promisee. (We still have to stop and think each time to remember who is the mortgagor and who is the mortgagee.) In the land of the lawyers the dead woman is the testatrix, the logic follows ipso facto, and the mayor's freedom from responsibility is his sovereign immunity. The same fellow who argues at home opines, maintains, and advances in the office.

If long words are unavoidable, old ones are disembalmed and used by lawyers who want to impress. In 1976, the District of Columbia updated and amended this archaic statute governing waste by a tenant (failing to maintain a premises):

> A man from henceforth shall have a writ of waste in the chancery against him that holdeth by law, or otherwise for term of life, or for term of years, or *a woman* in dower; and he which shall be attainted of waste, shall lease the thing that he hath wasted, and moreover shall recompense thrice so much as the waste shall be taxed at [emphasis added].[5]

What changes were made, you wonder? The words *a woman* were removed. The rest stayed as is. How modern the legislative draftsmen are in the nation's capital.

In a case involving nothing more metaphysical than charges of fraud against a stockbroker, the defendant's lawyer wrote this piece of literature in his brief: "The duty owing from defendants to plaintiffs in the abstract will vary, under White, relative to the juxtaposition of the real world environmental encasement of the two sides. The concept of causation would seem less plastic." The appellate judge commented plaintively on this passage in a footnote to his opinion: "Briefs should be written in the English language."[6]

Amen!

IV. Forget the Windup; Just Make the Pitch

Just say what you mean to say. Do not lead in to every thought with prefatory puffery. It is standard legalese to waste several lines of lead-in before getting to the point. This needless language clutters the message, as when judges write that they "have read all the briefs, carefully considered the lawyers' arguments, pondered the applicable law, and related it to the facts of the case," et cetera. Must they so assure their audience, lest it be assumed that they have reached their decision without careful research, without attention to all that transpired, and without giving it their best effort? We all presume they did their homework; telling us they did only makes us suspect they did not. This kind of rhetoric is self-conscious and self-serving. It persuades no one and takes up space needlessly. Here is one such introductory windup that took three full printed lines of space to lead into the essential half a line.

> Having considered the situation and interests of the parties, the relevant statutes, the nature of the contract and all of the circumstances surrounding it, the Tribunal concludes that *the claimant was hired on an annual basis.*

All the context required was the last half line: "The claimant was hired on an annual basis."

A similar windup occurs in this sentence: "After carefully considering the pleadings and testimony in this case as well as the public policy concerns, the court concludes that the sale should be set aside." "The sale should be set aside" would have been enough. That was what everyone wanted to know: the decision.

A variation on the above theme is the unduly solicitous phrases lawyers often use to describe their colleagues. "The case made by my estimable opponent that . . . ," or "This honorable court is respectfully urged to exercise its infinite wisdom and. . . ." Some of our friends on the bench tell us that whenever they see themselves called "learned" in a colleague's opinion, they know they have lost their point. These references are as phony as they are unnecessary. Cut them out. "The defense argues" or "the highest court held" are adequate.

Omit words like "it is urged that" before a simple statement that stands better alone, such as "the confession should not be admitted into evidence." Professor Rodell referred to these legalistic statements as examples of the backhanded passive: "it would seem to appear that" or "it is suggested that." They are local to legal writing and should be discarded.

Another example is the arm's length windup: "it is observed at the outset that," "turning to the next point, it is believed," or even "we proceed on the assumption that. . . . ," "these points will be considered. . . ." Donna Woolfolk Cross calls this kind of writing "the one-legged subjunctive, a favorite trick that helps lawyers plant both their feet firmly in midair."[7] These are gambits to avoid commitment, as if the writers could escape blame for a bad judgment by refusing to make themselves the subjects of a sentence. Whether its purpose is to effect modesty or to avoid accountability, the "it would seem" school of writing should be shunned. Write in the active voice, and be declarative: just observe, turn to, consider, find, or whatever it is you as the writer are promising to do. Do not hold yourself at literary arm's length with these wordy windups.

To cure this problem simply edit away all superfluous introductory phrases. "It is evident that . . . ," "as stated earlier . . . ," "as we have indicated," "under the circumstances of this case . . . ," "it should be noted in this regard that. . . ." We came across this comment in one lawyer's brief: "The issue may be oversimplified by the following, but I think Brevity of the issue presented may establish the simplicity of the legal concept of liability which the Plaintiff fully believes is appropriate." Our favorite cliché is: "Not wishing to belabor the point, it should be repeated that . . ."; the writer then went ahead and belabored the point.

We also recommend leaving out remarks that are obvious or implicit. For example, in most situations it should not be necessary to add the words "under the circumstances of this case" or "it is my opinion that." Usually it is obvious that the opinion you are reporting is your own, and that it has to do with the facts detailed elsewhere in the document.

The prolonged windup arises in one other instance. It is the situation where judges overload their sentences with unnecessary authorial intrusions. "We think we are entitled to take notice of . . ."; "We first recite the well-established rule that . . ."; "In a statement which, to me, goes to the heart of the matter . . .";

"Since I have concluded that the tract in question. . . ." Prune them and your writing will become more decisive, tighter, less subjective, better.

This rule has its exceptions. At times you must distinguish your views from another's, and not to use personal pronouns would be awkward. If eight members of the Supreme Court rule one way, the dissenter could properly note that fact and point out that "I disagree with this interpretation." To say this any other way would result in clumsy writing. A Canadian judge, feeling obliged to avoid the first person at any cost, once wrote that "This court cannot hear the case because the court will be in another court at the time." The trick is to steer a middle course between embarrassing autobiography and writing bereft of personality.

Too many personal references to yourself in your writings can cause negative reactions in your readers. Generally, it is preferable to avoid references to yourself. It is not your personal view anyone cares about, as a rule. Rather, it is the position you represent (court, counsel, whatever) that is relevant. Often personal references in legal writing undermine the writer's authority. If you write "It is my opinion that the petition should be granted," or "I am satisfied that petitioners have established the requirements for issuance of the writ," your readers will be inclined to wonder just who you are that your opinion and your satisfaction should have weight. The same statements made objectively, as if you were deciding rather than pontificating, not calling attention to yourself, read far better: "The petition should be granted"; "The petitioners have established. . . ."

Forget the windup. Decide what you wish to say; then say it.

V. Avoid Purple

Purple prose is overly colorful and dramatic language. It is a flaw to which all writers succumb. It is art taken to the extreme, fancy footwork that ends up tripping the dancer. It includes overly colorful writing, misused metaphors, malaprops, and clichés.

Florid writing impresses the intellectual lightweight as high-class literature. To the critical eye, it is laughable.

This flamboyant excerpt comes from the Pennsylvania Supreme Court opinion of Justice Michael A. Musmanno in the obscenity case concerning the book *Candy*.[8]

The Supreme Court of Pennsylvania had an opportunity in this case to unlimber some heavy artillery in fighting for American morality; it had unlimited freedom to pour devastating fire into the forces that would destroy the very foundations of decency, purity and wholesome conduct upon which our American society is founded; it had the clearest chance to draw from the armory of the law the weapons which would beat back those who, for greed and lucre, would poison the minds of the youth of our Commonwealth. The Supreme Court, however, did none of these things. The Majority of this Court retired from the field of battle without firing a shot. It did more. It encouraged the foul foe to smash more effectively at the bastions of American decency; it unfurled a flag of impeccability and authority over the invading filthy battalions; it supplied to each hoodlum in the putrid expeditionary force a bar of Ivory Soap which made him, according to the Majority's reasoning, 99½ percent pure!

And later in his dissent, criticizing the U.S. Supreme Court for not enunciating clear principles in this case of the law:

Those decisions are a lighthouse with broken beams. The majority opinions of the present U.S. Supreme Court, on the subject of obscenity, constitute a never-never land of confusion and self-contradiction. Taken in the aggregate, those opinions suggest a region hazy with drifting fogs, beset with contrary wind currents, crisscrossed with labyrinthian, tortuous foot trails, perforated with pitfalls and tortured with quicksands, which no legal traveler could hope to traverse and emerge therefrom with a precise knowledge as to where he had been, what he had seen, and where he was now going.

These were his concluding words:

From all this we conclude that the Majority of this Court, by taking into the chamber of consideration and consultation an arithmetic table, a block, an ax, and circular logic, arrived at the conclusion that there could be no use in waiting to see what the Supreme Court might say in *Candy*, and thus, with a circular saw, it sawed away the rights of the people of Pennsylvania to be saved from the inundation of filth gushing from the pages of a book which the Majority finds possesses a minimum of social importance but never explains why.
Because, of course, it cannot!
From Pittsburgh to Philadelphia, from Dan to Beersheba, and

from the ramparts of the Bible to Samuel Eliot Morison's *Oxford History of the American People* [*sic*], I dissent!

A New York judge topped Musmanno with his opinion in a case involving an escaping bandit, a runaway taxi, and some injured pedestrians.[9] The 3½-page opinion is either a model of literary horsefeathers or the best put-on we have found in the published opinions of America's courts. Here is an excerpt from Justice Carlin's statement of the facts of this case:

> This case presents the ordinary man—that problem child of the law —in a most bizarre setting. As a lowly chauffeur in defendant's employ he became in a trice the protagonist in a breath-bating drama with a denouement almost tragic. It appears that a man whose identity it would be indelicate to divulge was feloniously relieved of his portable goods by two nondescript highwaymen in an alley near 26th Street and Third Avenue, Manhattan; they induced him to relinquish his possessions by a strong argument ad hominem couched in the convincing cant of the criminal and pressed at the point of a most persuasive pistol. Laden with their loot, but not thereby impeded, they took an abrupt departure and he, shuffling off the coil of that discretion which enmeshed him in the alley, quickly gave chase through 26th Street toward 2d Avenue, whither they were resorting "with expedition swift as thought" for most obvious reasons. Somewhere on that thoroughfare of escape they indulged the stratagem of separation ostensibly to disconcert their pursuer and allay the ardor of his pursuit. . . .[10]

The judge's prose did not improve when he got to the legal analysis. For example, he disposed of the plaintiff's argument that his client's right to be protected while he walked the public streets was superior to the cabdriver's right to abandon his taxi when he was in distress, in these immortal words:

> To hold thus under the facts adduced herein would be tantamount to a repeal by implication of the primal law of nature written in indelible characters upon the fleshy tablets of sentient creation by the Almighty Law-giver, "the supernal Judge who sits on high." There are those who stem the turbulent current for bubble fame, or who bridge the yawning chasm with a leap for the leap's sake or who "outstare the sternest eyes that look, outbrave the heart most daring on the earth, pluck the young sucking cubs from the she-bear, yea,

mock the lion when he roars for prey" to win a fair lady and these
are the admiration of the generality of men; but they are made of
sterner stuff than the ordinary man upon whom the law places no
duty of emulation. The law would indeed be fond if it imposed upon
the ordinary man the obligation to so demean himself when suddenly
confronted with a danger, not of his creation, disregarding the likelihood that such a contingency may darken the intellect and palsy the
will of the common legion of the earth, the fraternity of ordinary
men—whose acts or commissions under certain conditions or circumstances make the yardstick by which the law measures culpability or
innocence, negligence or care.[11]

Purple passages come from both sides of the bench. Here is an
attorney for an injured lumberjack launching into an overwritten
memorandum of law pertaining to a malpractice suit, first with a
flourish of traditional legalese, and then with an ornate apology for
the bad prose yet to come:

COMES NOW the Plaintiff, by and through his undersigned attorney, and respectfully submits the following Memorandum of Law
to the Court saying:. . . .[12]
    The case law of elective surgery first discussed in the quiet passages
of a doctor's office well known to the patient, selected by the patient,
is not the case in question. It is within the framework of that short
passage of facts that this Brief is written. In anticipation of some
surprise, I readily admit that many portions of this Brief are cynical
and factitious in remarks. Your writer assures this Honorable Court
that such passages are made for the purposes of emphasis and outrage
of modern society's failure to recognize the factual and, thereby, legal
interrelationships of the hospital and its patient.[13]

In his attempt at fancy writing, the lawyer sounds like Nathan
Detroit or some Runyonesque character trying to sound intelligent
by using unnatural language.
    The melodramatic and the mixed metaphor is a favorite of the
fancy writing school.

Husband and wife own an estate in entireties as if it were a living
tree, whose fruit they share together. To split the tree in two would
be to kill it and then, it would not be what it was before when either
could enjoy its shelter, shade and fruit as much as the other.[14]

It would be difficult to conceive of a durable umbrella with a greater diameter and circumference to protect Kenneth Polley from financial claims . . . and falling down upon all parties involved in its tragic periphery, than this release.[15]

To erect fire hydrants close to a dwelling is to assure the inhabitants of those homes that potential fire engines stand guard to fight an invading conflagration. To erect fire hydrants and then not inspect them with some reasonable regularity is like setting sentinels and then offering them no relief or food so that they fall over from exhaustion and thereby become useless as watchful guardians. . . .[16]

Throughout the entire history of the law, legal Jeremiahs have moaned that if financial responsibility were imposed in the accomplishment of certain enterprises, the ensuing litigation would be great, chaos would reign and civilization would stand still.[17]

In the latter case, by way of contrast, one of the judge's colleagues wrote this straightforward and clear concurring opinion:

I concur in the result because the complainant alleges negligence in the failure to inspect the hydrants and to replace or repair inoperative valves and in allowing the water in the hydrants to freeze.[18]

One judge, a former Rhodes scholar who attended our writing course, made this epic comparison in one of his opinions: "If this were a true statement of the doctrine, then the unruly horse of public opinion would be joined in the stable by a steed of even more unpredictable propensities." Another of our students wrote, melodramatically and unsuitably: "The death knell of the motion for continuance was sounded. . . ."

A law student wrote a memorandum of law to his professor that contained this opening:

Shelter is one of man's three essentials. The other two being, of course, food and clothing. America may be the land of the free and the home of the brave, but for some of the brave buying or renting shelter in certain areas can be an arduous, if not impossible, venture. It is not the intent of this paper to delve into the numerous sociological reasons behind this. We are concerned here with the means and the ends, not the cause. Suffice it to say that the melting pot concept has not come true due to some people closing out (or if you prefer, closing themselves in) other people from obtaining housing in the near vicinity to them. It's not often that you hear, over the din of clinking glasses at a cocktail party, "Some of my best friends are right next door," to paraphrase a cliché. . . .

Here is his conclusion:

> HOPE SPRINGS ETERNAL IN THE BIASED BREAST
> So long as Pandora's box remains closed, hope springs eternal in the human breast and the biased are no exception. The law has said nothing about discrimination against a person for reasons other than the now repetitive race, color, religion or national origin. So if you happen to dislike short actors who happen to be Whigs, well . . . go right ahead and refuse to sell or rent to them without fear.

The law student sent the paper to a prospective employer as a writing sample. Guess whether he got the job.

The malaprop—from the French *malapropos* (inappropriate)—is another example of the purple foible. John Ciardi defines it as "the incommodious subsidization of one word in lute of another, as in making a parsing reverence to allegories sunning themselves on the banks of the Nile."[19]

The malaprop is another laughable result of lawyers making literary leaps beyond their skills. Like the mixed metaphor, it results in such wincers as Judge Carlin's fleshy tablets and shuffling coils that enmesh, former Justice Musmanno's perforated pitfalls and traversable quicksands, and the scrubbed case underpinnings, guised fog, and interlined creases of the following opinion in a recent District of Columbia sex discrimination case:

> Those subtleties—inextricably woven through any form of prejudice—particularly interline the creases of age where victims of discrimination, actual or apparent, represent the more vulnerable, sensitive members of our society.
> The Court then is especially wary of the nuances of action and word and discerns whether, overt expression to the contrary, they in fact signify any form of age discrimination. In this climate each case, supported by its own underpinnings, must be scrubbed clean of the fog of discriminatory obfuscation creeping in "on little cat feet" in the guise of economic priority.[20]

Clichés are another shade of purple. They may be useful in informal communication, but they make writing seem trite. Thus, a recent presidential report included this ominous message: "However, a forward-looking follow-through does not flow easily from even the most careful historical backswing."

That mouthful should be worth fifty dollars from *The New Yorker*.

If you find purple prose irresistible, get it out of your system by writing it; then edit it out. It won't hold up to the light of day. You will be embarrassed by it later.

VI. WRITE CONCISE, CLEAR, SIMPLE WORDS, SENTENCES,
    AND PARAGRAPHS

William Strunk, Jr., and E. B. White explained the need for conciseness:

> Vigorous writing is concise. A sentence should contain no unnecessary words, a paragraph no unnecessary sentences, for the same reason that a drawing should have no unnecessary lines and a machine no unnecessary parts. This requires not that the writer make all his sentences short, or that he avoid all detail and treat his subjects only in outline, but that every word tell.[21]

Ernest Hemingway made the same point in *The Sun Also Rises*. The subject was bullfighting, but the message applies to writing:

> Romero never made any contortions, always it was straight and pure and natural in line. The others twisted themselves like corkscrews, their elbows raised, and leaned against the flanks of the bull after his horns had passed, to give a faked look of danger. Afterward, all that was faked turned bad and gave an unpleasant feeling. Romero's bullfighting gave real emotion, because he kept the absolute purity of line in his movements and always quietly and calmly let the horns pass him close each time. He did not have to emphasize their closeness.[22]

Conciseness and simplicity are essential to good legal writing, too. In legal writing, particularly, the need for clarity is paramount. It is incorrect to argue, as some do, that law is different from literature in its demands upon language. Here, for example, is an excerpt from an artfully written opinion by Justice Oliver Wendell Holmes in a case questioning the constitutionality of a state sterilization law.

The attack is not upon the procedure but upon the substantive law. It seems to be contended that in no circumstances could such an order be justified. It certainly is contended that the order cannot be justified upon the existing grounds. The judgment finds the facts that have been recited and that Carrie Buck "is the probable potential parent of socially inadequate offspring, likewise afflicted, that she may be sexually sterilized without detriment to her general health and that her welfare and that of society will be promoted by her sterilization," and thereupon makes the order. In view of the general declarations of the legislature and the specific findings of the court obviously we cannot say as matter of law that the grounds do not exist, and if they exist they justify the result. We have seen more than once that the public welfare may call upon the best citizens for their lives. It would be strange if it could not call upon those who already sap the strength of the state for these lesser sacrifices, often not felt to be such by those concerned, in order to prevent our being swamped with incompetence. It is better for all the world, if instead of waiting to execute degenerate offspring for crime, or to let them starve for their imbecility, society can prevent those who are manifestly unfit from continuing their kind. The principle that sustains compulsory vaccination is broad enough to cover cutting the Fallopian tubes. Three generations of imbeciles are enough.[23]

Conciseness, as this example shows, is not telegraphese. A concise sentence may in fact be quite long. But like Romero's bullfighting, it has the elegance of simplicity, as does this powerful passage from Robert H. Jackson's closing address as prosecutor in the Nuremberg war trial. The words were spoken, of course, but they read as elegantly as the best literature.

The Nazi movement will be of evil memory in history because of its persecution of the Jews, the most far-flung and terrible racial persecution of all time. Although the Nazi Party neither invented nor monopolized anti-Semitism, its leaders from the very beginning embraced it, incited it, and exploited it. They used it as "the psychological spark that ignites the mob." After the seizure of power, it became an official state policy. The persecution began in a series of discriminatory laws eliminating the Jews from the civil service, the professions, and economic life. As it became more intense it included segregation of Jews in ghettos and exile. Riots were organized by Party leaders to loot Jewish business places and to burn synagogues. Jewish property was confiscated and a collective fine of a billion marks was imposed upon German Jewry. The program progressed in fury and irresponsibility to the "final solution." This consisted of sending all Jews who were fit to work to concentration camps as slave laborers, and all who were not fit, which included children under twelve and people over fifty, as well as any others judged unfit by an SS doctor, to concentration camps for extermination.[24]

Of course this rule can be exaggerated. If writing is too abbreviated, it will read like a message from Tonto. We do not urge extremes. We do endorse the rule. In good writing, as in Bauhaus architecture, less is more.

VII. PUNCTUATE PRECISELY
Punctuation is akin to street signs in a strange town. Without them, the visitor will get lost. Not only does punctuation make writing correct, it also removes troublesome ambiguities. Poor punctuation or the absence of punctuation can lead to expensive mistakes, costing money and even lives. A comma can completely change the meaning of a sentence. Imagine the damage a court reporter could cause by mispunctuating the following sentences:

    a. The prisoner said the witness was a convicted thief.
    b. The prisoner, said the witness, was a convicted thief.

Courts take a balanced view of the impact of questionable punctuation on legislation. Ordinarily they will not construe laws contrary to the conventions of punctuation unless the punctuation makes the law absurd, inconsistent or ambiguous.[25] *American Jurisprudence on Statutes*[26] goes further, stating that in the interpretation of laws punctuation "is not seriously regarded," is a "minor, not a decisive or controlling element," "is a fallible standard" of meaning, and is "the last resort as an aid in interpretation." If the legislature's true meaning is manifest, courts will not let punctuation determine interpretation. But all cases dealing with punctuation acknowledge that the conventions are an aid in interpreting doubtful provisions of laws and will be considered where it is provident to do so.[27] Books on statute construction state this rule,[28] and courts generally follow it.[29]

The U.S. Supreme Court has said repeatedly that punctuation "is not part of the statute,"[30] "no part of an act" of Congress.[31]

To get the "true meaning of a statute, courts read with such stops as are manifestly required."[32] Despite this impressive authority, and some state laws that punctuation shall not control or affect statutes, "attorneys continue to wrangle and worry over punctuating; and courts occasionally defend and justify their decisions with commas —absent or present or misplaced."[33] Thus while not a part of statutes, the arbitrary marks of punctuation serve important functions, and "no draftsman of statutes can afford to disregard the subject."[34]

A federal court in Pennsylvania,[35] for example, followed the balanced approach in a case involving a cigarette smoker's claim that he got lung cancer because of a tobacco company's breach of warrants. At issue was the interpretation of one section of the Pennsylvania Sales Act of 1915, which followed the Uniform Sales Act except in an instance where ambiguity was caused by one period and one comma. It was argued that the punctuation caused one phrase to modify an antecedent clause, and thus changed its meaning. The federal court refused to accept this argument, holding that in cases of statutory construction, punctuation may not determine the intention of the legislature. In Pennsylvania, the practice was for the legislature to pass bills and send them to the governor without punctuation, which was inserted later by the secretary of the commonwealth. He had no legislative power to affect meaning in carrying out his limited ministerial, executive functions. The court "freed" itself from the commas and construed the law as it understood the law was intended to be.

A federal court in Maryland faced a similar claim, but had no legislative history to guide it, nor any case law.[36] The defendant was indicted for possessing counterfeiting paraphernalia. One section of the statute was awkwardly worded, and the defendant questioned whether a clause set off by a comma modified a preceding clause. The court decided the case based on its own reading of the statute, holding that the defendant's contention made no sense. Any other reading would have made the statute meaningless, and the court refused to do this.

Courts will decide cases on the basis of rules of punctuation where the law is ambiguous; if it is not, courts will not undo a clear and sensible law by blind compliance with rules of grammar or punctuation.[37]

In cases between private parties, courts will apply a test of reasonableness to interpreting disputed writings and will resolve ambiguities against the writers. This is what one federal court did in a dispute over the coverage of an insurance policy regarding injuries sustained in an elevator.[38] In analyzing the punctuation of the disputed provisions, the court admonished that "it would not have required extraordinary skill for the authors of this policy to clearly express the meaning they asked" the courts to find in the policy. The insurance company blamed the lawyers who wrote their policy.

Another federal court refused to accept the views of an insurance company's expert witness (an English professor with a Ph.D.) regarding the coverage of an insurance policy.[39] Acknowledging that "punctuation can tend to affect meaning otherwise unclear," the court said the expert's conclusion was "far afield" from the "sense of the subject matter," which was clear and unambiguous to the court.

Not only does punctuation itself cause problems such as the ones we mentioned earlier, it can also lead to poor sentence structure, which creates other problems and makes for poor reading. If the following paragraph from a lawyer's brief had been divided into several sentences, it would have been much clearer.

A prenuptial agreement between Mr. J and the deceased dated June 8, 1971, a copy of which was introduced into evidence as petitioner's exhibit no. 6, declares their intention, in consideration of the marriage, that their property acquired prior to marriage should be enjoyed and disposed of as sole and separate property of each of them and after death of either his property should be free from any claim by the other on account of community property laws in the same manner as if the marriage had never been celebrated.

Put periods after the "1971" in line 2, "no. 6" in line 3, and "them" in line 5, and add a few words to make the sentences complete, and you have made an obscure paragraph clear.

The following paragraph from a jumbled legal opinion could have been clarified by making the two awkward sentences into four orderly ones. Here is how we found it.

Premeditation should not, as the majority herein seems to do, when their opinion holds that the design or intention to kill need not have preexisted for any definite time, be treated as synonymous with intent. Intent, unlike premeditation, is also one of the elements of second-degree murder and intent must be accompanied by a deliberate preconceived plan to kill in order to raise the degree to the highest level of murder.

Here is how we would change it, leaving the author's language essentially as it is, but punctuating it differently.

Premeditation should not be treated as synonymous with intent. This is what the majority opinion does by holding that the design or intention to kill need not have preexisted for any definite time. Intent, unlike premeditation, is also one element of second-degree murder. In order to raise the degree to the highest level of murder, intent must be accompanied by a deliberate preconceived plan to kill.

One test of correct punctuation is to read the writing aloud. If you lose your breath before coming to the first period, or if the sentence sounds long-winded and confusing, start over. This test will flag overloaded sentences like the following excerpt from a civil trial appeal:

It appears from the record that J.C.P. was either a daughter or a niece of R.P. and we conclude that the trial judge's instruction to the jury that the mere statement by the grantors in the deed that they were heirs did not necessarily mean that they were children, that "they could be nephews, cousins" prevented the error, if any, from being a reversible one when considered alone or when considered with the erroneous admission of the obituary notice.

In urging that the trial judge should have granted their motion to strike the trial setting, the appellants say that the appellees were not correct when, under Local Rule 3 of the H. County District Court, they certified in requesting the trial setting that the pleadings were in order and that all matters preliminary to trial had been accomplished; that the trial court erred in overruling the motion to strike the setting because this provision of the rule should have been applied.

The two paragraphs above suffer from lack of punctuation, incorrect punctuation, and the questionable replacement of punctuation with conjunctions. If at the end of line 2, for example, the word "and" was replaced with a period, the sentence would read well. So would the two following sentences if the comma in line 4 was replaced with a period.

The case for correct and precise punctuation does not need to be exaggerated. We acknowledge that the conventions of punctuation are somewhat uncertain and arbitrary. Standards vary and change. Nevertheless, the guideposts we recommended are neither the fetishes of petty printers nor the exotica of fussy English teachers. They are the accepted current conventions. They are aids in assuring comprehensibility and clarity—important in any legal document.

Punctuation is not a science, the conventions change, and the rules will not always be deemed by courts to be dispositive of cases. Still, there are important reasons for lawyers to pay careful attention to punctuation. If they do not, their opponents will. And their clients may, too. The lawbooks are loaded with cases that hinged on punctuation. And not all disputed cases go to court; the number of costly disputes caused by questionable punctuation can never be completely tabulated. To the degree that lawyers write to promote stability and certainty, and to guide important action—that is, to arrive at clear understandings—they must watch their punctuation lest it undo what they set out to accomplish.

VIII. Use Other People's Written Work
    Incidentally and Deftly

Most legal writing contains other people's writing—citations of relevant authorities, quotations from trial records, authoritative books, statutes, and judicial opinions. Many of these sources are themselves examples of barbarous writing. Attorneys generally think that frequent long quotations give their work the appearance of scholarly authority; actually, excessive use of poorly written sources adopts and compounds other peoples' incompetencies.

a. *Citations*

The practice of citing authorities is a scholarly tradition in legal writing. The reasons for it are obvious, and we do not question the practice itself. But we do question the practice of dropping whole chains of titles and numbers right in the middle of a sentence, interrupting the reader's train of thought, forcing the eye to jump back over the citation to the earlier text, build up momentum, and leap over the citation to the rest of the sentence while the idea coheres. For example:

The freedom of religion provisions of the First Amendment, applied to the states through the Fourteenth Amendment, *Cantwell* v. *Connecticut*, 310 U.S. 296, 60 S.Ct. 900, 84 L.Ed. 1213 (free exercise clause), *Everson* v. *Board of Education*, 330 U.S. 1, 67 S.Ct. 504, 91 L.Ed. 711 (establishment clause), prohibit the civil courts, as well as the legislatures, from injecting themselves into ecclesiastical disputes. *Kreshik* v. *St. Nicholas Cathedral*, 363 U.S. 1980, 80 S.Ct. 1037, 4 L.Ed.2d 1140. See *Kedroff* v. *St. Nicholas Cathedral*, 344 U.S. 94, 73 S.Ct. 143, 97 L.Ed. 120.

By the time the reader scans two lines of legal citations, the thought preceding them has become faint and the idea following the citations seems disconnected. We find ourselves going back to the beginning, rereading the first lines, and then leaping over the citations to the rest of the text while the idea is still fresh. If the sentence above was divided into two shorter sentences, covering the two separate ideas, the citations would appear where they belong: at the end of each sentence, not in the middle of one.

Another version of the same problem arises when citations are used to introduce a sentence. Consider this example from a Kentucky opinion:

In *Taulbee* v. *Commonwealth*, Ky., 201 S.W.2d 723 (1947), and *Murphy* v. *Commonwealth*, Ky., 279 S.W. 2d 767 (1955), this court held that in a prosecution for the offense of taking a motor vehicle without the consent of the owner, the refusal of an instruction on drunkenness is not error. Those cases are dispositive here.

The paragraph would read better if the first two lines, the citations, were used at the end of the first sentence, before the second sentence, which really refers to the prior citation. The first sentence could start with the words "In similar cases, this court held. . . ."

When the citation is included at the end of a sentence, the revision is even more obvious and simpler. "The Ohio Supreme Court disposed of the question decades ago; therefore, the defendant's claim is governed by that court's decision in *Roe* v. *Doe*, 48 Ohio 202 (1930)." Why not put a period after the word "decision," then add the citation?

The worst example of this foible is the repeated use of intermittent citations throughout a sentence. Too frequently, one will come across a sentence like this prototype in a brief, an opinion, or a law review article:

> The constitutional principle is clear, *U.S. Constitution, XIV Amendment,* Section I, that whether courts are reviewing the propriety of a fine in a criminal case, *Williams* v. *Illinois,* 399 U.S. 235 (1970); *Tate* v. *Short,* 401 U.S. 395 (1971); or the question of excessive money bail, *U.S. Constitution, VIII Amendment,* also see *Stock* v. *Boyle,* 342 U.S. 1 (1951); *U.S.* v. *Bandy,* 81 S.Ct. 197 (1960), or even the access of impoverished defendants to adequate defense counsel, *Gideon* v. *Wainwright,* 101 L.Ed. 1041 (1962)—indeed there are countless comparable examples in the cases, see, e.g., Jones—*New Directions of the Fourteenth Amendment,* 100 Yale Law Journal 555 (1980), that states may not deny "the equal protection of the laws" to people by discriminating against them on account of their poverty.

By the time the reader plows through this dense thicket, deflected along the way by the interrupting citations, the thought is lost. Needless to say, the constitutional principle referred to in the beginning of this belabored sentence is not so clear as the author promised at the start.

One last point about the use of citations. Use the ones you need, not every one you have come across. Many lawyers succumb to the understandable tendency to show off how much research went into their work by blitzing the reader with long strings of citations. It is almost as if they are saying to the reader: "I went to the library last night and read cases for four hours. Now I'm going to overwhelm you with my scholarship."

This tactic has the opposite effect. It shows the reader that the writer cannot discern, select, and weigh the relative values of cases. It diminishes the potency of the real, select gems, which are tossed into the mass and lose their impact. And it bores and annoys the reader. A boss (senior partner, judge, research director, client) is not necessarily impressed with the fact that his employee can overload a memorandum of law with citations to hundreds of cases. It is interesting to know that there are hundreds of cases on the point in question, but the boss probably wants to know the particular handful that truly decide or govern the issues under consideration.

The same is true of public writings. The readers of a judicial opinion or of an article or book, or the judge reading a long brief, may be pleased to have a catalogue of cases on a point of mutual interest, but they do not want this list of cases to encumber the reading material. Put the citations at the end. Then the reader who is not interested can ignore them, and the reader who is interested can use them. Writing laden with extraneous material interrupts the process of reading.

We do not question the use of citations in text, for they are often necessary. We urge they be used unobtrusively, which usually means placing them after the end of the sentence to which they refer.

The citation always works best at the end of the sentence; when it doesn't, there is reason to suspect that the sentence is too long. Sometimes citations can wait until the end of the paragraph, or even the end of the page. A good general rule is to use citations at the latest point where they can be used without affecting the integrity of the text and the citation. Placing the citation so it does not interrupt the text always improves the writing and makes it easier to read.

b. *Quotations*

Basically, the writer should keep quotations to a minimum. Like the overuse of citations, writers like to show what they know by adding boundless quotations from their research. Heaping gobs of quotes onto a piece of legal writing accomplishes the opposite of what is intended. Readers do read short quotes, but they tend to jump over or speedily scan long quotes, especially when there are lots of them in a piece of writing.

The line that separates scholarship from plagiarism may be thin and vague. It cannot be avoided by overattribution, using large patches of someone else's work but noting that it is theirs with quotes and citations. More than incidental use of someone else's work diminishes the freshness and uniqueness of your own.

There may be a good reason to quote some lines from an opinion, a statute, a trial record, or occasionally from a nonlegal source such as a poem or play. But it ought to be because it says something better than anything else could, or because it goes to the heart of the matter in question. But this criterion is met infrequently.

The writer can use an eye test to determine if there are too many quotes or if infrequent quotes are too long. Scan the full writing. If it is peppered with quotes, see whether most of them could be eliminated or paraphrased in your own words. Then see if the quotes that are used could be shortened by cutting out or paraphrasing unimportant parts. If you see a quotation running on for pages or monopolizing pages or even paragraphs, edit until this is not the case.

One cause of long quotations is convenience: it is far easier to have your secretary copy long passages from statutes, opinions, and other documents than it is for you to reduce those passages to their essence. Good writing, however, is always more convenient for the reader than it is for the writer. Synthesize, select, do your own writing, and use only necessary quotations. If the case concerns a question of construction, quote only the words or the few words or sentences at the heart of the case, not the whole statute or documentary provision. If another court's decision is the last word, use the key word or phrase or sentence. Do not quote whole paragraphs or pages. If an excerpt from a record is central to your point, use it. Do not unroll page after page of it verbatim.

In the cases of both citations and quotations, consider them materials gathered by an artist. Do not simply pile them all together. Choose, discard, sculpt, shape the necessary pieces, and then work them into your overall design. Be deft and subtle. The extra work will pay off.

IX. CHECK WRITING AUTHORITIES

There are general writing authorities, such as the dictionary and the thesaurus; and there are specific ones, such as the government or corporate or academic manual that governs your office's writing style. Use them. Keep them close by, and resort to them regularly.

Get into the habit of looking up words. You will discover that more often than you might have guessed, you used the wrong word or a remote or strained version of the one you should have used. Lawyers who put on airs frequently get themselves into semantic trouble.

Imprecise language, the unwitting use of a not quite right or downright wrong word, is a common flaw in legal writing. The result is sloppiness, at best; at worst, it results in errors in the substance of the law. Mark Twain said that the difference between the right word and the almost right word is the difference between lightning and the lightning bug. William Wordsworth said that the difference between prose and poetry is that prose is the perfect word in the perfect place, and poetry is the most perfect word in the most perfect place. We would hold lawyers to no more rigorous a standard than that they use the correct words in the proper places.

In addition to your general reference books, you also should use the special authorities on style that are unique to your work—for example, the Government Printing Office manual on style,[40] which tells all government lawyers what the preferred styles are (e.g., to spell federal with a capital F). Like it or not, you must follow the formats of your particular job.

The Harvard Blue Book[41] is another authoritative style manual lawyers should use. There may be no reason for you to memorize the rule for using *Ibid.* and *Id.* in your footnote citations, but there also is no good reason for you not to have the generally accepted sourcebook of all these rules and to use it.

X. Edit One More Time

All professional writers will attest to the truth of former Justice Louis Brandeis' adage that there is no such thing as good writing— there is just good rewriting. The habit of self-editing is difficult to develop. Lawyers are busy people; therefore, they tend to be done with their writing at the first opportunity. That is an excuse, a lazy rationale for avoiding the hard and painful work of editing their own writing.

In addition to shortages of time, there are psychological impediments to self-editing. Once words are committed to paper, especially when they are in print in a clean copy, it is painful to make changes. Good writers must learn to rewrite, delete, and change their prose.

Cut and paste. Remember, your last draft is not etched in stone; it is always possible to make changes. A polished piece of writing is a result of hard work. The notion that good writers casually dash off dozens of pages in the heat of an inspiration and that we read it later exactly as it poured from their pens is a romantic fantasy. Good writers edit compulsively.

There is no precise instant when a piece of writing is ready the way we know a soufflé is ready. Every time you go back to edit your writing you will find ways to improve it. Writers cannot take this lesson to the extreme, or they would never be done, and nothing would ever be published. The habit we want to encourage is rewriting as much as possible.

The more time you allow between writing and editing, the more likely you will see opportunities for improvement. Distance permits a more critical view.

The lawyers who have taken our writing course are asked as a final assignment to take something they have written and liked, and to edit it again, one more time. The results are always impressive. Invariably they confirm the usefulness of this tenth commandment. Nothing illustrates our point better than an edited piece of writing, blue-lined and cut by the author, proudly, to a fraction of its original size.

Remember that what you write may be your legacy. Give it as much care as you can.

A California judge recently criticized his judicial colleagues for the "galloping prolixity" of their "welter of words."[42] He lamented that judicial opinions were becoming a "vanity press" for the judges to publish their "ego trips" to the dismay of their captive audience. Appellate judges never use one authority when twenty are available, he exhorted; we enshrine the written word, we rediscover the obvious, enhance the trivial, mollify losing counsel and the lower court, and make redundancy triumph.

"If Moses were a justice of a reviewing court today," he wrote, "the Ten Commandments would emerge in several bound volumes complete with pocket parts and supplements." Legal opinions, this iconoclastic judge wrote, should be understandable by the world that is asked to comply with them. We agree with his admonition: "We must remember that we are not Delphic Oracles emitting mysterious and enigmatic axioms to be comprehended and explained only by the temple priesthood—lawyers and other judges."

Notes

Introduction: Let's Kill All the Lawyers

1. Fred Rodell, "Goodbye to Law Reviews" 23 *Virginia Law Review* 38 (1937), at 38; also see "Goodbye to Law Reviews—Revisited" 48 *Virginia Law Review* 279 (1962).
2. Fred Rodell, *Woe Unto You, Lawyers* (New York: Pageant Press, 1939), introduction by Jerome Frank.
3. Anthony Lewis, *Gideon's Trumpet* (New York: Random House, 1964).
4. Charles Rembar, *The Law of the Land* (New York: Simon and Schuster, 1980).
5. Edmond Cahn, *The Moral Decision* (Indianapolis: Indiana University Press, 1955).
6. Sybille Bedford, *The Faces of Justice* (New York: Simon and Schuster, 1961).
7. Ephraim London, ed., *The World of Law*, Vols. I and II (New York: Simon and Schuster, 1960).
8. Louis Blom-Cooper, ed., *The Literature of the Law* and *The Language of the Law* (New York: Macmillan, 1965).
9. *Woe Unto You, Lawyers*, p. 127.
10. The Bar Association of the City of New York has published a list of selected materials on the subject of plain-language laws. The literature in this field is growing. Two Washington, D.C., organizations—Americans for Legal Reform and the American Institutes for Research—have followed this movement and report on it regularly in their bulletins. The subject is one of increasing popularity around the country, and there is considerable reform activity throughout the states.
11. Graham Hughes, "A Mixed Bane," *New York Review of Books* (March 9, 1981), p. 16.

1 Legalisms, Latinisms, and Macaronics

1. Ritter, "Latin Lives in Legal Language," 63 ABA *Journal* 1512 (1977).
2. "A Primer of Opinion Writing, for Four New Judges," 21 *Arkansas Law Review* 197 (1967).
3. 66 ABA *Journal* 679 (1980).
4. *The New Yorker*, 97 (August 21, 1981).

2 Correctness: Reminiscing about the Future of the English Language

1. Lloyd v. Vermeulen, 22 N.J. 200 (1956).
2. Guiseppi et al. v. Walling, 144 F.2d 608 (2 Cir. 1944).
3. Waters v. Quimby, 27 N.J.L. 296, at 311.
4. T.I. McCormack Trucking Co. v. U.S., 251 F.Supp. 526, at 533 (1966).
5. U.S. v. Shirey, 359 U.S. 255 (1958), at 260, 261.
6. People ex rel Whipple v. Saginaw Circuit Judge (1873), 26 Michigan 342, at 344–345.
7. People v. Hallberg, 259 Ill. 502, 102 N.E. 2d 1005 (1913).
8. Ibid.
9. Petty and Evans v. Colorado, 156 Colo. 549, 400 P.2d 666 (1965).
10. Covington v. Peo, 36 Colo. 183, 85 P.832.
11. Dunn v. Perrin, 570 F.2d 21 (1 Cir., 1978).
12. Bahm v. Pittsburgh & Lake Erie Rd. Co., 6 Ohio St. 2d 192 (1966).
13. Hughes, *The Supreme Court of the U.S.: Its Foundation, Methods and Achievements—An Interpretation* (New York: Columbia University Press, 1936).
14. Cahn, "Justice Black and First Amendment Absolutes: A Public Interview," 37 *N.Y.U. Law Review* 549 (1962).
15. Black, "The Bill of Rights," 35 *N.Y.U. Law Review* 865 (1960).
16. NLRB v. Miller, 341 F.2d 870, at 874 (1965).
17. Iowa–Des Moines National Bank v. Insurance Co. of North America, 459 F.2d 650 (8 Cir. 1972).
18. Coney v. Rockford Life Insurance Co., 67 Ill. App. 2d 395 (1966).
19. Lo-Vaca Gathering Co. v. Missouri-Kansas-Texas Railroad Co., 476 S.W. 2d 732 (Texas Civ. App. 1972).
20. Ibid. at 737.
21. Hogya v. The Superior Court of San Diego, 75 C.A. 3d 122 (1977).
22. Commissioner of Internal Revenue v. James B. Kelley et al., 293 F.2d 904 (5 Cir. 1961).
23. Connecticut Light and Power Co., initial decision as to F.P.C. jurisdiction, August 19, 1975, by Administrative Law Judge Convisoer, at p. 20.
24. Lo-Vaca Gathering Co. v. Missouri-Kansas-Texas Railroad Co., supra.
25. Susie Green v. First National Bank of Tuscaloosa, 49 Ala. App. 749, 272 So. 2d 904 (1973).
26. Ibid.
27. Gertrude H. Block, "Should the English Language Have a Sex Operation?" 40 *Illinois Quarterly* 24 (1977).
28. American General Insurance Co. v. Webster et al., 118 S.W. 2d 1082 (Tex. Civ. App. 1938).
29. James Patton et al. v. Royal Industries et al., 263 C.A. 2d 760 (1968).

30. *Webster's Third New International Dictionary* (Springfield, Mass.: G. and C. Merriam Co., 1961).
31. Chicago Steel Foundry Co. v. Burnside Steel Foundry Co., 132 F.2d 812 at 814 (7 Cir. 1943).
32. Ibid.

3 Punctuation: Who Can Hang by a Comma?

1. Ala. Const., Art. XVIII, (section) 284.
2. Cassidy et al. v. Vanatta's Ex'r et al, 242 S.W. 2d 619 (Ky. Ct. Appeals, 1951).
3. Sawyer v. State of Maine and Sheriff Sharpe, 382 A.2d 1039 (Sup. Jud. Ct. Maine 1978).
4. See *Employment Practices Decisions*, Vol. 8, 9854, at p. 6548 (1974).
5. Oral opinion of Judge Howard S. Chasanow, 7th Judicial District of Maryland, in Maryland v. Jos. Parker, case no. CR-4293, delivered on May 15, 1979.
6. I. Shenker, "Dash It All—There's a Punctuation Controversy," *New York Times*, March 19, 1978.

4 Organization: Procrusteans and Butterflies

1. Terminiell v. City of Chicago, 337 U.S. 1, at 2 and 3 (1949).

5 Style: A Dancer in Chains

1. Oliver Wendell Holmes, "The Path of the Law," in *Collected Legal Papers* (New York: Harcourt, Brace and Company, 1921), p. 175.
2. Wagner v. International Railway Co., 232 N.Y. 176 (1921). Reprinted in *The Language of the Law: An Anthology of Legal Prose*, Louis Blom-Cooper, ed. (New York: Macmillan, 1965), p. 340.
3. Bain Peanut Co. v. Pinson, 282 U.S. 499, 501 (1931).
4. People v. Defore, 242 N.Y. 13, 21, 150 N.E. 585, cert. denied, 270 U.S. 657 (1926).
5. Brewer v. Williams, 430 U.S. 387 (1977).
6. Ibid. Chief Justice Burger's dissent appears at 415–429.
7. Reprinted in *The Language of the Law*, p. 91.
8. Ibid. at pp. 349–350.
9. E. B. White, *Stuart Little* (New York: Harper & Row, 1945), p. 102.
10. Earl Warren, "Inside the Supreme Court," 239 *Atlantic*, 35, 39 (April 1977). *The Memoirs of Earl Warren* (Garden City: Doubleday, 1977), p. 291.
11. E. B. White, "Death of a Pig," *Essays of E. B. White* (New York: Harper & Row, 1977), pp. 20–21.
12. From the *Cornhill Magazine*, 7 (1863), reprinted in *The Language of the Law*, p. 64.
13. Carl Sagan, *The Dragons of Eden: Speculations on the Evolution of Human Intelligence* (New York: Random House, 1977), p. 13.

14. Olmstead v. United States, 227 U.S. 438, 471, 485, 48 S.Ct. 564, 575, 72 L.Ed. 944 (1928).
15. *The Language of the Law*, pp. xvii–xix.
16. Ibid. at p. xix.

6 Before and After

1. Greenbaum, "Lawyers Talk Too Much," 19 *Federal Rules Decisions* 229, at 235 (1956).
2. Irving Kellogg, "How To: A Plan for Drafting in Plain English," 56 *California State Bar Journal* 154 (April 1981).
3. Ibid. at 159.
4. We were assisted in this editing assignment by Washington attorney David Astern and University of Michigan professor Dwight Stevenson.
5. During the legislative year 1977–78, 804 federal laws were signed by the President and 44,319 state laws were enacted (*Book of States, Council of State Governments*, 1980–81 edition, at pp. 104–105; Legislative Office, U.S. House of Representatives computerized report). Obviously, many more bills were written than were passed.
6. Elwork, Sales, and Alfini, *Making Jury Instructions Understandable* (Charlottesville, Va.: Michie/Bobbs-Merrill, 1981).
7. Charrow and Charrow, "Making Legal Language Understandable: A Psycholinguistic Study of Jury Instructions" 79 *Columbia Law Review* 1306 (November 1979).
8. By 1980, forty-three out of fifty-two states and all federal courts had adopted standard instructions, according to scholars. *Making Jury Instructions Understandable*, at p. 26, citing R. G. Nieland, *Pattern Jury Instructions: A Critical Look at a Modern Movement to Improve the Jury System* (1979).
9. Charrow and Charrow, "Making Legal Language Understandable," p. 1306.

7 The Ten Commandments of Legal Writing

1. Elliott v. Dollar General Corp. et al., 475 S.W. 2d 651 (S.C. Term 1979).
2. George S. Kaufman and Morrie Ryskind, *Animal Crackers* (1928).
3. Donna Woolfolk Cross, *Word Abuse—How the Words We Use Use Us* (New York: Coward, McCann, & Geoghegan, 1979).
4. Mellinkoff, *The Language of the Law* (Boston: Little, Brown, 1963).
5. 45 D.C. *Code Encyclopedia* 1301 (West).
6. Gottreich v. San Francisco Inv. Co., 552 F.2d 866, at 867 (1977).
7. *Word Abuse*, p. 41.
8. Commonwealth v. Dell, 427 Pa. 189, 233 A.2d 840 (1967), cert. denied, 390 U.S. 948, 88 C.Ct. 1038, 19 L.Ed. 1140 (1968).
9. Cordas et al. v. Peerless Transportation Co. et al., 27 N.Y. Supp. 2d 198 (1941).
10. Ibid. at 199.
11. Ibid.

12. Sanders v. Putnam Community Hospital, Case No. 78-690 CA, Cir. Ct. Putnam County, Florida.
13. Ibid.
14. Sterrett v. Sterrett, 401 Pa. 583, 166 A.2d (1960).
15. Polley v. Atlantic Refining Co., 417 Pa. 549, 202 A.2nd 900 (1965).
16. Doyle v. South Pittsburg Water Co., 414 Pa. 199, 199 A.2d 875 (1964) at pp. 878–879.
17. Ibid. at p. 884.
18. Ibid. at p. 885.
19. *A Browser's Dictionary: A Compendium of Curious Expressions and Intriguing Facts* (New York: Harper & Row, 1980).
20. Kerwood v. Mortgage Bankers Association of America, Inc., Dist. Ct., D.C., C.A. No. 79-0889, June 24, 1980.
21. William Strunk, Jr., and E. B. White, *The Elements of Style*, 2nd ed., (New York: Macmillan, 1972), p. 17.
22. Ernest Hemingway, *The Sun Also Rises* (New York: Charles Scribner's Sons, 1926, 1970), pp. 167–168.
23. Buck v. Bell, 47 S.Ct. 584, 585 (1927).
24. "Closing Address in the Nuremberg Trial," in *The World of Law*, E. London, ed. (New York: Simon and Schuster, 1960).
25. Baker v. Morrison, 86 So. 2d 805 (S.C. Fla. 1956).
26. 50 *Am. Jur.* 250, Statutes, S.253, p. 249.
27. Baker v. Morrison, supra at 867; Hamford Produce Co. v. Clemmons, 412 S.W. 2d 828, at 837 (S.C. Ark., 1967).
28. 50 *Am. Jur.* 250, Statutes, S.254, 82 *C.J.C. Statutes*, S.341, p. 685, *Crawford, Statutory Construction* (1940), Horack's Sutherland, *Statutory Construction* (3rd), Vol. 2, S.4939.
29. For example, Broward Builders Exchange v. Goehring, 231 So. 2d 513 S.C. Fla. 1970).
30. Hammock v. Loan & Trust Co., 105 U.S. 77 (1881).
31. U.S. v. Shreveport Grain & Elevator Co., 287 U.S. 74, 82 (1931).
32. U.S. v. Lacher, 134 U.S. 624 (1890).
33. Brossard, "Punctuation of Statutes," 24 *Oregon Law Review* 157 (1945), p. 158.
34. Ibid. at p. 158.
35. Pritchard v. Liggett & Myers Tobacco Co., 350 F.2d 479 (3 Cir. 1965).
36. U.S. v. Dixon, 446 F. Supp. 236 (1978).
37. Allen v. Adami et al., 347 N.E. 2d 890 (1976), dissent at 893.
38. McNally v. American States Insurance Co., 308 F.2d. 438 (6 Cir. 1962). Courts will strictly construe zoning regulations, too, in favor of property owners. See Allen et al. v. Adami, 347 N.E. 2d 890 (N.Y., 1976).
39. Community National Bank in Mammoth v. St. Paul Fire & Marine Insurance Co., 399 F. Supp. 873 (S.D. Ill., 1975).
40. U.S. Government Printing Office Style Manual, GPO 021-000-00070-1, rev. ed.
41. *A Uniform System of Citation*, Harvard Law Review Association, 12th ed., 4th printing, 1978.
42. R. Gardner, "Toward Shorter Opinions," 50 *California State Bar Journal* 240 (June 1980).

Index

About the Authors

RONALD L. GOLDFARB was born in Jersey City, New Jersey. He attended Syracuse University, where he obtained his B.A. and LLB, and he holds LLM and J.S.D. degrees from the Yale Law School. He is senior partner at the law firm Goldfarb, Singer & Austern in Washington, D.C. His previous books include *Migrant Farm Workers: A Caste of Despair, Jails: The Ultimate Ghetto*, and *Crime and Publicity*. He has also written for such major periodicals as *The New Republic* and the *New York Times Magazine*. He lives with his wife and three children in Alexandria, Virginia.

JAMES C. RAYMOND was born in New Orleans, Louisiana. He holds a B.A. from Spring Hill College, an M.A. from the University of New Orleans, and a Ph.D. from the University of Texas. He is currently associate professor of English and assistant dean of the Graduate School at the University of Alabama. He is author of a previous book on prose style called *Writing (Is an Unnatural Act)*. He lives with his wife and two children in Tuscaloosa, Alabama.